RELIGIOUS EDUCATION DEP
LIGHT OF CHRIST

TEACHING SACRAMENTS TO YOUTH

Teaching
Sacraments
to Youth

by
Richard Reichert

PAULIST PRESS
New York / Paramus / Toronto

Library of Congress
Catalog Card Number: 75-9121

ISBN: 0-8091-1880-7

Published by Paulist Press
Editorial Office: 1865 Broadway, N.Y., N.Y. 10023
Business Office: 400 Sette Drive, Paramus, N.J. 07652

Printed and bound in the
United States of America

Contents

To you . . .
for having the generosity and convictions
necessary to communicate the mystery
of Jesus' continuing presence in our midst
to the young—and the old

Introduction

What and Why

The book is intended as an aid to persons—parents, volunteer teachers and professionals—who are involved in and concerned about introducing youth to our sacramental tradition and fostering in them an appreciation of that tradition. As such it contains theology related to the sacraments both in the beginning overview chapter and throughout each unit or additional chapter. But it is theology that is hopefully "popularized," that is, presented in a language and in a logical progression that will make it more understandable to both teachers and students. It is "updated" theology in the sense that it tries to reflect the best of contemporary thinking regarding sacraments. It is "orthodox" theology in the sense that is rooted in the tradition and official teaching of the Church.

It is not, however, exhaustive. It does not try to pursue all the ramifications related to questions of sacramental theology. Rather it focuses on key issues, what might be called the essentials.

The book is also methodological. Each chapter contains a series of suggested activities arranged in logical progression as a means of introducing a topic to the students. Most of the activities are already "classroom" tested by the author. A few are original but

1

are based upon proved principles of method. In other words, the methods can work. There is no guarantee that they always will work in a given set of circumstances. They should be viewed with that kind of caution.

For Whom

The content and methods have been prepared primarily for students from junior high school (7th grade) through high school. Many of the methods, however, can also be used with adult groups and as a form of teacher training. With adults, of course, there will be a need to make minor adjustments in some instances. The book is geared principally for use in either formal or in CCD settings. With some adjustments many of the activities can be used by parents teaching their own children. Even if some of the activities can't be used by parents, the ideas presented and the manner in which they are presented should be helpful.

How To Use the Book

It is intended to be a complete course. That is, it progresses from basic concepts to more specific information about sacraments in a logical (and psychological) fashion. At the same time individual chapters could be used independently of others, since each is in one sense a complete unit in itself.

The format for each chapter contains an Introduction, usually with some background information, regarding the objectives of the unit. This is followed by a Beginning, activities for initiating the topic; the Next

Step, activities for continuing the topic; and finally the Heart of the Matter, activities for focusing in on the central theological concern of the topic.

Some alternate activities are suggested in each of these parts in case the main activity seems inappropriate. One word of caution. The suggested activities should be viewed as aids rather than essentials. If you feel uncomfortable with a particular activity, it is advisable to drop it and develop one of your own with which you feel comfortable. The activities suggested in the book should serve at least as a starting point for thinking up ideas for an alternate activity.

Each activity is designed to be the basis for one class or session. It is possible, however, to do several activities in a session. It is also possible to continue the discussion initiated by the activity into a second or even third session. Too, a combination of these activities could serve as the basis for a weekend or overnight program.

In short, everything presented has been developed with an eye to flexibility and practicality. It should be possible to adapt the various chapters to just about any teaching situation.

One final idea. Nothing teaches liturgy better than the liturgy itself. For that reason every attempt should be made to build into the schedule opportunities for celebrating Eucharist together, for celebrating the Sacrament of Forgiveness, for participating in baptisms or other sacramental celebrations on occasion. If we take the definition of sacrament as presented in this book seriously (guaranteed opportunities for encountering Jesus through ritual celebrations) the wise teacher will provide as many of these opportunities as possible and let the sacraments speak for themselves, or rather Jesus speak for himself.

1. Overview of Sacramental Theology

Its fairly common to hear obstetricians remark that no matter how often they have delivered babies, each new birth is a continuing marvel to them. It puts them in intimate touch with the whole mystery of life and they never cease to be amazed. This is no less true for the parents involved and for the immediate relatives. A birth is always a significant event pointing to deeper realities and to the very mystery of life itself. It is a profound experience for all involved.

In a real way we can call such an event a kind of sacramental experience. Used in a broad sense, a sacramental experience is anything that puts us in contact with deeper realities and ultimately with God. For that reason theologians generally refer to sacrament today as an encounter, a coming into contact with God. Experiencing such an encounter has an effect on us. It changes us. We view ourselves and all reality a little differently as a result. Our behavior or life style is changed.

Particular persons can have somewhat the same effect on us. Just being in the presence of a holy person, a gifted artist or a persuasive leader can have a profound effect on us. By being in contact with the person we are somehow put in contact with realities we normally do

not recognize. It is in that sense theologians refer to
Jesus as the sacrament of encounter with God. Through
Jesus persons were placed in the presence of the Father.
Through Jesus they encountered the Father. Their lives
were changed as a result. In much the same way the
Church is referred to as a sacrament. By being in touch
with the living faith community a person can be placed
in contact with God. The presence and action of the
faith community point to a deeper reality and ultimately to God. The Church is a sign or a sacrament of
God's presence among men and his saving actions in
our behalf.

The word sacrament as used by theologians today
therefore has what might be called a general meaning.
It is virtually any event, person or thing with the capacity to reveal to us the deeper realities of our existence
and ultimately sacrament has the capacity to put us in
touch with God, to encounter God, to experience God
who is always present but not always recognized.

Using sacrament in this broad sense we can say
that the Hebrew experience of Exodus, their escape from
the slavery of Egypt was a sacramental experience.
Through it they discovered how powerful, how loving,
how intimately concerned Yahweh was in their welfare.
Through the event itself they encountered, discovered,
recognized Yahweh in an entirely new way and their
whole history was altered as a result. In a similar way
various leaders and prophets had what might be called
a sacramental effect on them. Persons like Isaiah put
them in contact with God, revealed God's presence and
his will. As a result, the words and actions of Isaiah
were recorded, reflected upon and continued to have
importance to each new generation.

One way of viewing the whole Old Testament is to

see it as a record of all the sacramental events and pro-phetic persons within the history of the Hebrew people. Creation itself has a very sacramental dimension. The Flood, the call of Abraham, the conquest of the Prom-ised Land, the reign of David, even the Babylonian Captivity had a certain sacramental character for the Hebrew people and continued to have such a character for the early Church Fathers.

So when we speak of sacrament it is important first of all to understand the term in its broadest sense as any event, person or thing with the capacity for re-vealing God to us and enabling us to encounter him.

In Church circles, though, the term sacrament usually has a much more specific meaning. It generally refers to one of the seven ritual sacraments which are an essential part of the Church's life. To understand a ritual sacrament an analogy might help. We referred to the birth of a new child as having a certain sacramental character. It is a profound experience that puts us in touch with the very mystery of life. Celebrating the child's birthday a year later with a little cake and one large candle in a gathering of relatives and friends is our attempt to recall and through certain signs mean-ingful to us re-present the original mysterious event. We do several things in the process. We look backward to the past event, we celebrate the present moment of life, we look forward to the future. We do all this through commonly accepted words, objects and ges-tures. The song, the cake and candle, making a wish—these are rituals commonly accepted in our culture for recalling and re-presenting the original event. In the process something of the original event is re-ex-perienced, especially by the mother and father. They are placed once again, even though in a low key way, in the presence of the mystery of life and the mystery of procreating life. Any ritual sacrament, then, has its roots first of all in an original sacramental encounter with God. A ritual sacrament is a people's conscious attempt to recall, re-present and therefore re-experience the original encounter with God.

It is for this reason that the Jewish people to this day still celebrate the Paschal meal each year. It is their ritual recalling and re-presenting that sacramental experience of God's love for them that their ancestors experienced several thousand years ago when rescued from Egypt. In that ritual re-presentation, the Jewish people can even today come into contact with, encounter the God of their ancestors.

We can see, then, that while there is something absolutely unique about the seven ritual sacraments of the Church—we will look into this shortly—we would be naive to think that sacramental experiences and the ritual re-enactment of those experiences are something exclusive to the Catholic Church.

Virtually every religion known to man had its origins in what might be called sacramental experiences or encounters with God. Virtually every formal religion today includes ritual re-enactments of those original experiences. While the religions might not view those rituals as sacraments in the same way the Church regards its own sacraments, they nevertheless have a certain sacramental character, a capacity to put people in touch with the God they have discovered.

What makes the Church's sacraments different, what gives them their unique character, is Jesus. First, Jesus in his person is the fullest revelation of the Father we humans can experience. He is the sacramental experience par excellence. His presence, his words, his deeds

and ultimately his death-resurrection far exceed anything else man has experienced in terms of direct encounter with God. Second, when the Church recalls and
re-presents through ritual signs, the key actions of Jesus
on earth, he becomes present in those very signs. It is
his presence under the ritual signs that gives the
Church's sacraments a qualitative difference, makes
them unique, totally other in character from the ritual
celebrations of other religions. This is not intended as a
"put down" of other religions since their rituals have an
integrity and a validity that flow from the original sacramental experiences that gave birth to those religions.
Those rituals can provide the worshipers with an encounter with God. We are only saying that since it was
in Jesus that God became most fully present to man
and since Jesus is present whenever the Church ritually
re-presents his words and actions, it is the presence of
Jesus that makes the difference.

Again an analogy may help to clarify this important point. The birth of a new baby is obviously a much
more profound experience for the parents than for the
six-year-old brother or sister of the infant. So when it
comes time to celebrate the infant's first birthday, that
ritual will have much more meaning for the parents
than for the six-year-old child. In other words, the
more profound and authentic the original experience,
the more meaningful will be the ritual re-enactment of
that experience.

If we apply this to certain primitive religions, we
can say that the primitive people's experience of God,
though valid, was somewhat limited. As a result they
arrived at limited and often distorted notions about God.
It would follow that in any ritual re-enactment of
events through which they had originally discovered

God, the ritual would itself provide only a limited and distorted experience of who God is for them.

On the other hand, Jesus, through his presence, his words and his deeds is God's fullest revelation of himself. It would follow necessarily that the Church's ritual re-presentation of Jesus' words and deeds, a re-presentation in which Jesus actually becomes present to us again, will provide a more perfect encounter with God than that experienced in the rituals of non-Christian religions.

In saying that, of course, we're begging the question. I couldn't "prove" what I just said. It rests on convictions arrived at through faith. The believers in other religions are equally convinced that their experience of God and the consequent rituals they celebrate are authentic. So the intention here is not to "prove we're right." Rather, we just want to see our own sacraments in as broad a perspective as possible. Ritual sacraments are not unique to the Catholic Church. Other religions have them even if they do not name them or describe them quite as we do. What is unique for us is our belief that Jesus is Lord and that he is the fullest revelation of God to man. That belief is what gives our ritual celebration of the seven sacraments their uniqueness. What we recall and re-present through signs are the words and actions of Jesus. Through those signs Jesus himself is present and acts. It is our belief in who Jesus is that gives to those rituals a uniqueness found nowhere else in the history of man or in man's religions.

We have said a great deal in a few pages. Let's go back now and examine in more detail some of the key ideas about the nature of sacraments. Since this book is intended to be functional rather than speculative, it will be more useful to list these key ideas in "text book" fashion.

1. A SACRAMENT IN THE BROAD SENSE IS ANY EVENT, PERSON OR THING THROUGH WHICH WE COME INTO CONTACT WITH, ENCOUNTER, EXPERIENCE GOD IN A NEW OR DEEPER WAY THAN PREVIOUSLY EXPERIENCED.

The important distinction here is between "sacrament in a broad sense" and the seven ritual sacraments of the Church. In this broad sense, virtually any event or person can have a sacramental effect on us. A sunset, a period of quiet prayer, an intimate conversation with a close friend—any of these things has the potential for revealing God to us in a new and deeper way. This does not mean this always happens.

On the one hand some events and situations are more "charged" with God. For example, our reference to the birth of a baby. That event brings us much closer to the mystery of God and his life-giving love than does a round of golf. The impact of first viewing a spectacle such as the Grand Canyon is likely to be more charged with sacramental dimensions than a walk through a city park. So while God can certainly be discovered everywhere in his creation and in the events of our daily life, it is safe to say that God will be more fully revealed in certain aspects of creation and human life than in others.

On the other hand our own receptivity, our sensitivity, our capacity and openness to "see" play a real part in all this. The ultimate openness, of course, is our faith, our capacity to "see" God in Jesus. But there is a more general openness in terms of our everyday life. For example, two persons can view the Grand Canyon at the same time and come away with entirely different impressions. The father, tired, cranky and hot after driving all day with a car full of noisy children is less likely to "see" what some relaxed young couple would "see" when viewing the same canyon. An unwed father is likely to view the birth of his child quite differently from some happily married man.

Besides these circumstantial differences which affect a person's ability to "see," there are what we might call habits or patterns of behavior. Some people have never cultivated this sensitivity to the sacred as revealed in nature and human events. Others have developed this sensitivity to such a high degree that even the most simple objects like a wild daisy or the most ordinary event like the excitement of the young child can awaken an experience of God's loving presence.

Given these two qualifications—some events are more charged with God's presence than others and people vary in their capacity to "see" God in these sacramental manifestations—we can recognize on the one hand why certain events in the history of Israel were more significant than others. At the same time we can recognize why Jesus, the fullest manifestation of God to man, was received differently by different people. In much the same way we can recognize why certain events in our lives will be more significant to us than others, at the same time discovering the significance depends in a real sense on our own openness and receptivity.

2. A SACRAMENTAL EXPERIENCE IS AN EN—COUNTER WITH GOD.

While still using sacrament in the broad rather than ritual sense, we now want to focus on the concept of encounter. It means primarily a meeting between persons. We do not encounter the Grand Canyon. But if when viewing the Grand Canyon we experience something of the power and beauty and majesty of God and are drawn more closely to him, we call that an encounter. It is basically at a meeting between persons that we discover the other more deeply and are ourselves changed by what we discover.

Understanding encounter in this way we are distinguishing a sacramental experience from other human experiences, no matter how intense they may be. For example, an atheist could have a profound aesthetic experience while standing at the rim of the Grand Canyon, one that he might remember the rest of his life. But because he does not recognize God as a person, there can be no encounter with God for him in that experience. What makes human experiences sacramental encounters, is our openness to and discovery of the person of God in the experience.

Even while we believe in God it does not automatically mean every profound experience is a sacramental one. We, too, could stand at the rim of the Grand Canyon, marvel at its immensity and beauty and not once "see" God in the experience. It is important to keep this in mind. A truly sacramental experience is one in which we consciously grow in our awareness of God, his presence and his person. A sacramental experience is an experience of "seeing" God, touching him, achieving communion with him.

For example, it is possible for us to spend a great deal of time in the presence of another person, share many experiences with that person and yet never encounter that person. Then suddenly there's a moment when a word, a gesture, a gentle touch reveal to us in a flash a dimension of that person we never saw before. That's an encounter. We know the person in a new way and as a result that person affects our lives quite differently than before. These are special moments. These are gifts. In the same way, while we are always surrounded by God and while virtually every event is potentially sacramental, actual encounters with God could be relatively infrequent. One thing is certain; we know it when it happens. Another thing is also certain; our faith, that is, our openness to God is critical. Finally, even though our faith may be strong there is no way we can manipulate or program an encounter. They are always free gifts, free self-revelations by God.

3. ENCOUNTERS ALWAYS CHANGE US.

This would sound a little like magic except for one fact. The change effected is always chosen by us. In other words, an authentic encounter with any person demands a decision of us. We must either accept that person as now revealed to us or we must reject him. Either way our decision will alter our life. We become different persons every time we truly encounter another. This is especially true in terms of our sacramental encounters with God. The encounter demands a decision: either we must enter more deeply into relationship with God or we must draw further from him.

The grace of a sacramental encounter is always essentially the gift of God's presence and his invitation to a closer relationship. What we do with that gift and invitation is still ours to choose. No sacramental encounter automatically implies a change for the better. That would be magic and unfortunately has too long been a misunderstanding of the nature of the Church's ritual sacraments. Sacramental grace is the gift of God's presence as such. Our acceptance or rejection of the friendship it implies is what changes us.

For example, a couple may be dating for some time, enjoy each other's company and grow to know each other quite well. Then one evening the young man reveals to the girl in a special way his love for her and his desire to marry her. In this kind of encounter where one person offers himself to another we have both gift (grace) and invitation. The girl's response will be what changes her. One thing is for certain, their relationship will never be quite the same again. They will either grow closer together or begin to drift apart. So it is, at least to a degree, whenever we have a sacramental encounter with God. We will never be quite the same again.

In speaking of sacrament in the broad sense, then, we can summarize by saying virtually any event or person could provide us with an encounter with God by which we are changed. Does this in fact happen very often? Yes and no. In a low key way the faithful and especially the prayerful person will have these kinds of sacramental encounters regularly. But in terms of key points in our lives, what we can look back on as experiences that radically altered our entire lives—they aren't as common.

It is precisely for that reason that the ritual sacraments of the Church become so important to us. These are actions of the faith community that guarantee us the *opportunity* to encounter God.

4. THE CHURCH'S SEVEN RITUAL SACRA-
MENTS ARE GUARANTEED OPPORTUNI-
TIES FOR ENCOUNTERING JESUS AND
THROUGH HIM THE FATHER.

The first important word here is guaranteed. By it
we mean whenever the Church gathers with the conscious intention of ritually celebrating a sacrament,
Jesus will be present to that community. It is for this
reason the Church has always placed so much importance on the sacraments and their capacity to bring us
to holiness. At the same time, a misunderstanding of
what is meant by "guaranteed" has led the faithful at
various times in history to invest a kind of magical
power in the sacraments. For example, some still feel
that the earlier a person receives Confirmation the
greater the guarantee the person will have the "strength"
to withstand temptation. It is in this sense too that the
idea of quantity became more important than quality.
If participating in Eucharist once a week is good, daily
Eucharist must *automatically* be better.

That's why today theologians put much stress on
the word opportunities as opposed to guaranteed. What
is guaranteed is the opportunity to encounter Jesus.
There is no guarantee the encounter will in fact take
place since that depends on us, our faith and our
openness. For example, there is a big difference between going to Mass drunk and going to Mass sober.
Common sense tells us that. But there is also a big difference between Confirmation received by a well prepared and highly motivated young adult and Confirmation received by a ten-year-old not yet fully capable of
understanding what is happening or why.

Note, there is no denial that a ten-year-old could

experience something of an encounter with Jesus through reception of Confirmation. We are guaranteed of Jesus' presence within the ritual celebration. We are only saying that the ten-year-old's immaturity limits his capacity for any kind of personal encounter simply because of his own limited personal development. We'll have to come back to this point when we deal with the individual sacraments.

For now, let us just stress that the ritual sacraments are guaranteed opportunities for encounters with Jesus. They are not guaranteed encounters. This means essentially that we personally are involved and that our faith, attentiveness, openness, maturity and understanding all play a part in deciding if we will actually experience an encounter (the grace) that changes our lives.

5. THE RITUAL SACRAMENTS ARE RE-PRESENTATIONS THROUGH SIGN OF PARTICULAR ACTIONS OF JESUS.

This statement is loaded so we should break it down a little more. First is the idea of re-presentations. Another word might be re-enactments. On the one hand it implies a looking back to something in history, something objective, something that has already taken place. So a ritual sacrament has its roots in the past, in the words and actions performed by Jesus while on earth. For that reason, the rituals are not just arbitrary. The sacraments aren't things the Church dreamed up. On the other hand, the rituals have been developed by the Church. The Church chose particular signs, words, gestures out of many available to her as the means for re-presenting the particular action of Jesus. Throughout history these signs have been adapted to meet the circumstances in which the Church finds herself. For example, while water has always been integral to the ritual sacrament of Baptism at various times the re-presentation took the form of either pouring or total immersion. While bread and wine are integral to Eucharist, whether the bread is white or whole wheat, unleavened or leavened is not integral.

What is critical to ritual sacraments is not the variation in signs over the centuries. What is critical is that the Church consciously intends through the signs she does use to re-present or re-enact particular actions of Jesus.

6. JESUS HIMSELF IS PRESENT WITHIN THE RITUAL RE-PRESENTATION OF HIS ACTIONS.

The key concept here is present. Note we make no attempt to localize that presence. At Eucharist, for example, we can certainly say he is present in the signs of bread and wine, but he is also present in community's action of coming together, of singing, of sharing the kiss of peace. He is present in the reading of the Gospel. In the same way he is present in the pouring of water at Baptism, and in the act of anointing the sick with oil.

While the Church's emphasis on Jesus' real presence in the consecrated host and cup is hardly erroneous, an over-emphasis on that particular localized presence has in fact detracted from the people's understanding and recognition of Jesus' equally real presence at Baptism, at the exchange of marriage vows, at the celebration of Penance.

If we say all seven sacraments are guaranteed opportunities for personal encounter with Jesus, then Jesus is really present in the celebration and under the signs of each sacrament. To try to pin that "presence" down to a particular moment, set of words, gesture or object is in fact to limit one's opportunity for the desired encounter. For example, if one limits his opportunity to actually encounter Jesus at Mass to the precise moment when receiving the host, then the ritual sacrament would exist in that one act alone and nothing else.

In fact the ritual re-presentation of the action of Jesus consists of a combination of individual signs (objects, gestures, words) not the least of which is the community itself. It is the ritual seen in its totality that makes up the sacrament. It is the ritual in its totality that provides the guaranteed opportunity to encounter Jesus. It is one's absorption into, one's participation in the total experience that provides the encounter with Jesus.

Understanding ritual sacrament and the presence of Jesus in this way will help explain why theologians today do not spend as much time trying to explain how Jesus is present under the signs of bread and wine. It is not that theologians deny Jesus' presence. Rather they are encouraging us to view each ritual sacrament in its entirety and not in terms of isolated aspects. In this way we will have a much better chance of utilizing our guaranteed opportunity for encountering Jesus present.

7. THE SEVEN RITUAL SACRAMENTS RE-FLECT THE BASIC VALUES OF JESUS.

In all human society certain basic values seem to be universal: birth which represents entrance into community, coming of age within that community, communal sharing of all life as symbolized in the meal, peace and reconciliation within the community, marriage out of which new life is created for the community, concern for the sick and those about to leave the community through death, and the community's need for service to one another.

These basic human values obviously reflect the seven ritual sacraments. Throughout his own life on earth Jesus affirmed these values in both word and deed. He made them his own values, he helped men to understand them better, he performed actions which made it possible for men to achieve them. As we will see later, the seven ritual sacraments of the Church did not emerge full blown and carefully detailed overnight. In fact, the seven ritual sacraments took centuries to evolve and take their present rather precise form.

This does not mean the roots for these sacraments were not already present in the words and actions of Jesus. What is important is the fact that the seven sacraments as they have evolved re-present the basic values of Jesus. As we celebrate a particular sacrament we have the opportunity to encounter Jesus precisely in his act of affirming that particular value. In this way, we can say each sacrament has its own special or particular grace. Each sacrament provides the opportunity to encounter Jesus as he acts to help us realize a particular value in our lives.

For example, Jesus obviously placed great value on marriage and the family. When a couple ritually celebrates the sacrament of marriage, Jesus becomes present to them precisely as the Jesus who supports and loves and encourages the marrying couple. To encounter Jesus in this ritual celebration is to encounter him precisely as supporting the relationship of one to the other. It is to root the relationship in a shared encounter with Jesus himself. That is what makes Christian marriage a sacrament and not just a civil ceremony.

This same thing is true of each ritual sacrament. The seven sacraments viewed in their totality provide the Christian community with all the grace (opportunities to encounter Jesus) the community needs to maintain itself as a Christian community, that is, as a community which accepts, aspires to and lives by the values of Jesus himself. Through the seven sacraments the community continues to grow in the consciousness, the very life of Jesus. Through the sacraments the community receives and lives by the spirit of Jesus and his Father.

8. THE RITUAL SACRAMENTS, BY PROVIDING US WITH OPPORTUNITIES TO ENCOUNTER JESUS, BRING US INTO AN ENCOUNTER WITH THE FATHER AND BRING US UNDER THE GENTLE RULE OF HIS SPIRIT.

This last point should never be overlooked. Jesus' whole purpose and mission on earth was to bring us into the presence of his Father. In that encounter we come under his loving influence and thus begin to live by his spirit. The same continues to be true today. The seven ritual sacraments are intended as opportunities to encounter the Father *through Jesus*. It is ultimately the Father who redeems us and calls us to his Kingdom. It is ultimately the Father who forms us into community. In that way we can understand Jesus as the ultimate sacrament, the ultimate guaranteed opportunity to encounter the Father. The Church and the seven ritual sacraments take their origin and their meaning from Jesus and he sees himself ultimately as the means through which all men are led not to himself but to his Father.

In order to translate this rather brief overview of sacramental theology into something more manageable and useful for teaching to others and especially youth, our next step will be to take the ideas developed above and translate them into a series of short statements that hopefully will begin to make more sense. At the same time we will try to suggest some alternate words for actual classroom use since expressions like "encounter" are not what we normally consider everyday language. This list of concepts will make up what could be considered the basic content of a program of sacramental study for youth. In subsequent chapters we will present some way for actually developing such a program and explaining the particular concepts.

1. God can be discovered in just about any event, in other persons and in the things of nature.
2. Whenever we do discover God in one of these ways, we can call the event, person or thing that revealed God to us a sacrament or sign.
3. These discoveries always change us.
4. This discovering depends to a large degree on us— our willingness and ability to look, to be open, to be alert or attentive.

5. Most religions began when a person or group had a truly significant experience of God in such a sacramental way.

6. A ritual sacrament is a community's way of recalling, celebrating and therefore re-presenting the past sacramental experience.

7. Our Christian religion is founded on our ancestors' experience of discovering God in Jesus. His presence, his words, his actions and especially his death-resurrection were sacramental.

8. The Church's seven ritual sacraments are acts of recalling, celebrating and therefore re-presenting through signs particular actions of Jesus. These signs have been adapted by the Church over the centuries but remain essentially the same in purpose.

9. Jesus becomes truly present under these ritual signs used by the Church to celebrate a sacrament. Therefore, each sacrament is an opportunity to discover God, to be in touch with God in a special way.

10. These seven sacraments are rooted in the actions of Jesus and reflect the values Jesus held, recognized, affirmed and supported in the human community. Each sacrament affects the community's life in a particular way.

The above summary certainly doesn't exhaust sacramental theology. However, it does touch on the key issues with some emphasis on what today's theologians are presenting to us. It also stresses those dimensions of sacramental theology most likely to speak to the experience and the needs of youth. For that reason, before one actually begins to think about how to present some of these ideas, it might be good to review this chapter again. If possible, this is best done in discussion with other parents and teachers. The main purpose would be to identify concepts which appear to be unclear or which we have trouble accepting. Equally important, discussion provides the opportunity to attempt to put some of these ideas into one's own words and to couple them with personal meaningful examples. A familiarity, a confidence, a being comfortable with these concepts is very critical to success in trying to share insights and convictions with youth.

If we keep in mind that we are not trying to impart knowledge as much as a whole set of values, convictions and a life style, we can appreciate why the above concepts have truly to become a part of us before we can share them effectively with others.

While it would be possible to provide an extensive bibliography at this point, we will continue to be functional. Therefore, I recommend primarily the little book, *An American Catechism*, published by Chicago Studies in the Fall of 1973. Its section on "Sacraments," pages 312-364, is an excellent, accurate and thorough presentation of all the particulars related to sacramental theology. As a quick, dependable reference for seeking information on particular questions, I can't recommend it highly enough.

Having grappled with the ideas presented in this chapter and being armed with the little reference book just mentioned, there is no reason why a person could not venture into a classroom (or into a living room) and begin to share with youth our Christian heritage regarding sacraments. The following chapters will suggest some ways to proceed.

2. What Did You See?

Introduction

The purpose of this chapter is to explore ways of increasing students' general sensitivity to life around them and then to sensitize them to the possibility of discovering God in that life. Life here means events, persons and nature—their overall environment, their world. We will be dealing with the content implied in items 1-5 on pages 22-23.

The suggestions and comments that follow are geared primarily to teachers working in CCD settings or in classrooms with groups of six or more. However, many of the same approaches—at least the principles implied—can be used by parents in working with their own teenagers in a family setting.

I. *A Beginning*

Normally it does little good to approach youth with the announcement that: "Today we are going to begin studying the sacraments." It is much better simply to begin with an activity. While the activity itself should have some immediate purpose, there is no need at this point to relate it to your de facto overall purpose of studying sacraments. That can come later.

An example of the kind of activity I suggest as a

beginning would be to take the students out on the lawn, assign each a three square foot plot of ground, and tell them to observe "their land" for fifteen minutes in silence. Get to know the land, everything that lives and moves on it, its texture, smell, feel, etc. Ideally, you would have sufficient area to keep students relatively separated. An ideal situation would allow you to do this kind of exercise in a relatively "wild" place where there is more likely to be a large variety of insects, plants and the like.

When sufficient time has been allowed for their "survey," reassemble the students and invite them to share what they discovered. You can anticipate a wide range of responses varying from "nothing" to "'a whole world of life and activity I did not know existed." The latter response, of course, is what you are hoping to elicit since it provides the opening for your own comments. The main thrust of your comments would center on the fact that in just about every situation there is much more "happening" than we often notice. (Can anyone give some examples from his experience?) It takes a certain degree of willingness and practice to be really in touch with life around us. Some real obstacles found in our culture often prevent us from developing this kind of alertness or sensitivity. (Can anyone name some?) Is it really that important to have this kind of sensitivity? Why? How could we develop it? (Such questions could be presented as topics for a group discussion.) Before the end of the session, ask the group to suggest another kind of "field trip," some place or event they would like to observe together with the precise purpose of practicing this kind of sensitivity, this alertness to what is really happening around us.

The above is offered as a cursory example of what is meant by beginning with an activity involving sensitivity instead of a lecture about it. Besides being an example of how one could in fact begin a program of sacramental study I think it might be helpful to analyze it in terms of the principles of learning it implies. These same principles will be operative through the remainder of the book so it is best to identify them early:

1. As much as possible start from a common, immediate experience shared by the class. Often you will have to provide that experience.

2. Anticipate as much as possible the typical pitfalls and attempt to eliminate them. For example, just turning students loose on a lawn or in the woods is to court disaster. By assigning particular, relatively isolated plots and requiring silence *for the sake of the experiment* the exercise will have a reasonable chance for success. We cannot blame youth for acting like youth. But we can blame ourselves if we do not anticipate and channel their normal actions.

3. Be patient and flexible in eliciting comments following the activity. Give plenty of opportunity for responses. Do not be disappointed if you fail to get the desired responses. What is needed is a *natural* or *logical* opening for relating their activity to the ideas you wish to bring to their attention. Normally it will come if the activity has any validity at all.

4. As much as possible, keep students involved throughout by means of soliciting additional personal examples from them, directing questions to them, providing topics for group discussion.

5. As much as possible, involve them in helping, at least

in a general way, to plan the next session. You can maintain some direction and control by setting up limits (we do not have enough time to go downtown) or by providing several options and asking them to choose one (we could either do . . . or we could . . .).

Keeping these general principles in mind let us return to some other possible activities for beginning the program.

Identifying Sounds. In this activity ask all the students to remain absolutely silent and keep their eyes closed. They are to listen as carefully as they can to every possible sound they hear and try to identify as many different sounds as possible. Three to five minutes are enough time for this. Then solicit from the group as many different sounds as they heard. They could be listed on the board or newsprint if that seems helpful. By way of response the teacher would make comments similar to those in the example above about sensitivity, the need for practice, what happens when we are alert to what's happening around us.

Getting To Know a Rock. In this activity each student is provided with a small rock or large piece of gravel. They are given about five to ten minutes to get to know their rock (for a less mature group, ten minutes would be too long): how it feels, smells, tastes, its identifying characteristics, its "personality." Students are advised they should attempt to know their rock so well that they will be able to find it after it has been placed together with all the others on a pile in the middle of the room. A real master could find his rock in such a pile even with his eyes closed. When the getting acquainted time has expired, collect the rocks and put them in a pile. Invite volunteers to find their own rock (eyes closed is optional).

After all have had the opportunity to find their own rock, the teacher can initiate discussion by asking questions like: If we can in fact get to know even something like a rock, how come we seldom get to know so much of what surrounds us every day—persons, events, things? What would we have to do to become this aware of life around us? Again discussion and comments could move along lines of the first example.

With a little imagination a teacher should be able to develop an activity along the lines being suggested that would best suit the limits of the teaching situation (time, mobility, etc.). In any event, once the teacher feels the students have begun to get the general idea that there is a lot going on around us that we often miss and that being sensitive or alert to life is an important part of "being alive," the group is ready for the next step.

II. *The Next Step*

Here, concern is for moving from this basic sensory awareness of our surroundings to a kind of emotional, spiritual sensitivity. An ideal way to move the group in this direction (but one that is not always feasible because of time, transportation and the like) would be to take the entire group to a busy bus terminal, airport, shopping center or similar place where considerable activity is taking place. Students should be divided into groups of three. As groups they would pick a good place to stand and observe the situation. The idea would be for them to have at least a half hour for this, so one possibility is to ask the students to do this outside class time as a kind of "project."

When the groups are gathered together after their

field trip (as soon as reasonably possible, so impressions will be fresh) they are asked to share their observations. What did they see? Again, responses will vary from rather superficial observations to very perceptive ones. By perceptive I have in mind the observation of loneliness, great sorrow, or great joy (as when persons are being reunited), physical suffering, kindness or its opposite, greed, etc. From the various responses the teacher would gradually attempt to elicit from the group a consensus on the overall tone or mood of the place observed.

Having identified such a mood, perhaps loneliness, boredom or indifference (it need not be a negative mood, depending on what place was observed) the teacher has the desired opening for making personal comments like these.

With some sensitivity or alertness it is usually possible to discover beneath the externals of an event or situation a more intangible, rather spiritual reality. It is actually at this deeper level that human life is really taking place, but so often we miss it because we are not experienced in being attentive to this reality. Here it would be good to ask if the students can think of personal examples of how they experienced this deeper reality in a situation; for example, a time in which a person discovered beneath a friend's cheerful facade some deep hurt or sorrow. In this same context the teacher would ask students to share ideas as to why we often lack this kind of awareness and how it could be developed. It would also be good to ask the students to identify some of the situations where this kind of sensitivity becomes especially important, as in one's own family, with friends, in school and the like. This would serve as a good lead-in for a follow-up activity. Students could be encouraged to make their own "field trip" before the next class and report back what they observed. Hopefully they will discover more the second time.

If the field trip to a busy place is not feasible, the following alternatives could provide basically the same experience:

The Cafeteria as Lab. Here the same basic activity would be pursued but the teacher would use the school cafeteria as the place to be observed. Its immediacy has some obvious advantages.

The Newspaper as Lab. By providing each student with a copy of some newspaper, they would be asked to glance through it and attempt to identify an overall mood or tone the entire paper projects regarding their city. Using their responses and discussion as the starting point, the teacher would then proceed as described in the activity involving the field trip.

For parents working with their own children, any of the above are possibilities. In fact, the opportunity for informal conversation on this topic with the family is an ideal situation for achieving the desired goal of sensitizing the youth to the more emotional and spiritual dimension of life.

III. *The Heart of the Matter: Seeing Sacraments*

The amount of sessions spent on developing the kinds of sensory and spiritual sensitivity described above will vary from situation to situation. Some groups will move quickly; others will need or enjoy repeating or continuing certain activities several sessions in a row.

However, when the teacher thinks the group as a

whole is ready, the following activity will serve as an introduction to discussion on sacrament as such.

Provide each student with a grape, a leaf, a flower or some similar object. It is not necessary to have the same object for each student. In fact, variety is preferred. Recall to the students the earlier activity with the plot of ground or the rock and review some of the ideas about sensory awareness. This need not take too long. Ask the students to spend five-ten minutes examining their object as they had done in the early activity, but this time they should approach it from a somewhat different angle. The question they should continuously ask themselves is whether or not this object tells them anything at all about God. Can they "see" God through this object? What do they "see"? Encourage them to do this in silence and to try not to distract others.

When time has expired, ask for reactions. The ensuing comments should provide ample opportunity to find a logical place for the teacher to begin to focus on some of the key concepts of sacramentality such as the following. God can in fact be "seen" in even the simplest dimensions of creation. Whatever helps us discover him is what is called a sacrament, at least in the broad sense of the word. The sensitivity required to "see" God in such things is not quite like sensory awareness, but sensory awareness is a part of it. This sensitivity to the reality of God that can be discovered in the reality around us is often called prayerfulness. In another sense, what we often call faith is actually this kind of openness, this sensitivity to the reality of God.

At this juncture, it is good to ask students if they can recall any event, situation or thing from their past that seemed to have this sacramental character—an instance where they felt they had been "in contact with"

God. Or you might ask if they can think of events or things that seem to be more "charged" with God's presence than others. Normally some will make reference to church settings and in particular to one of the ritual sacraments. If they should, it is best to delay discussion on these saying something to the effect that they are unique and will be dealt with later. Keep the focus as much as possible on the sacramental potential in the life around them, since the main purpose here is to heighten this prayerfulness and openness to the sacred as discovered in their own lives.

Once students get at least some feel for what is meant by the sacramentality of the life around them and the kind of prayerful alertness involved, it is good to ask them if they would like to repeat one of the earlier exercises, namely observing a place or event to see if one can "discover" God in the bus station, cafeteria or newspaper. While this would be an optional follow-up to the present session, it does help at least to reinforce the overall concept. However, usually nothing too dramatic will be observed.

IV. *Open-Ended Ending*

In the following sessions the teacher will want to continue to pursue the overall topic. Several additional concepts should be introduced in these sessions:

(a) Scripture records some of the key sacramental experiences of the Jewish people—e.g., they discovered God in a new way through their Exodus experience. Other religions have similar experiences in their history.

(b) There are degrees to "discovering" God. Some

events in which we "see" God literally change our entire lives—e.g., a near fatal accident can do this. Some events, though important, have a less dramatic effect—e.g., viewing a particularly beautiful sunset or particularly violent storm gives us some "feel" for who God is.

(c) Different people will see different things in the same situation or event. Circumstances and/or faith account for this.

(d) All true experiences of God's presence do effect some change in us. That is, we are faced with a decision to draw closer to him or to move away from him. Ideas on the notion of personal encounter can be introduced now and students should be encouraged to share an experience of personal encounter they may have had with friends, relatives, etc.

How the teacher presents these concepts will vary. On the one hand, if the previous activities were very successful, students will be more open to direct presentation and the opportunity to discuss and to question. On the other hand, the concepts just mentioned might be better presented within the context of other activities, the viewing of an appropriate film (e.g., *The Late, Great God* by Paulist Films in connection with point c above) or in the context of a witness talk by a peer or adult. One important thing to remember is that any time spent developing this overall prayerfulness or sensitivity to God's presence in their lives will be worthwhile. It is not only an essential foundation for appreciating and participating in the Church's ritual sacraments. It is integral to the youths' overall spiritual development.

Also, the teacher should not resist being side-tracked—time permitting—into other topics that are suggested by this approach. For example, it could be beneficial, if the students express interest, to spend several sessions trying to identify and critique the sacramental experiences that are the basis for other religions (e.g., Mohammed's experience) and the key experiences of the Hebrews. In the same way, it would be invaluable to spend some time reviewing the Gospels and Acts to analyze how and why Christ was a sacramental experience to some and not to others.

For more sophisticated students, the whole question of the psychology of such religious experiences could be explored. When does imagination or neurosis end and authentic insight begin? While the teacher could understandably feel incompetent to deal with this question, if student interest is high, it would be good to invite a guest speaker who could deal with it. The ongoing principle here is that more effective learning takes place when we respond to students' present curiosity and interest.

We need not be in too great a hurry to get to our central concern, the Church's ritual sacraments, if what we do pursue is providing a good foundation for our future study. This is especially true when parents are working with their own children. The informality and flexibility of the ongoing relationship allows parents to move at their children's pace.

Another important topic suggested by this approach is that of prayer itself. To be sidetracked by students into this topic would truly be a happy delay.

In any case, a good way to end this whole unit on sacramentality is with a prayer service developed as much as possible by the students themselves. It has the value of fulfilling two purposes. First, it will serve as a good windup for this section. Second, it can provide a common experience to refer to as you move into the next section on the topic of ritual. The basic elements of such a service normally include a beginning song, followed by an appropriate reading from Scripture or other similar source. This would be followed by a few comments by the teacher or the student leader to identify the theme. Possible themes in this instance would be: Eyes To See and a Heart To Believe, Openness, Little Things, A Flower Is God's Face, etc. After introductory comments, it would be good here to repeat the earlier exercise wherein the students are given a leaf, flower, grape or similar object and asked to search for God by examining and reflecting on it. This would be done in silence for five-ten minutes. Some instrumental music could be played in the background. Next, students would be asked to offer spontaneous prayers in response to this experience. This would be followed by a short litany of thanks and petition composed ahead of time. The leader would read a statement like, "For always being so close to us" and students would respond, "Thank you, God." A number of these statements and/or petitions would follow and end with a short reading or a formal prayer. The entire session would end with a song.

This outline is just an example. The teacher and students could become much more creative. In any case, the prayer service should somehow incorporate and summarize the key concept of the sacramentality of the life around us.

The setting for this service is important as with any prayer service. Because of the overall theme, it might best be held outside in a natural, attractive setting. Otherwise the room used should be appropriately decorated with "sacraments" to help set the mood.

Having concluded this first unit, we are now ready to move on to the whole question of ritual and from there to ritual sacrament.

3. What Did You Say?

Introduction

Having awakened in the youth a general sense of the sacred and of the possibility for "seeing" God in the life around them, our goal in this unit is to develop in them a greater awareness of the role "man-made" signs and symbols play in communication between persons. For that reason, it seems good first to review some of the concepts involved.

Let us take as a useful example the instance of a man who comes up to us, hands us a cigar and says with a wide smile, "It's a girl!" What is happening is obvious. He is telling us his wife just had a baby girl. He is also communicating much more than that fact. He is communicating his own pride and relief, his joy and gratitude. Note, he does this with more than words. While words are one of the most commonly used "signs" man uses with which to communicate, each culture has developed others it also uses. Even if the man hadn't said "It's a girl," his gesture of handing out a cigar and his wide smile are common signs in our culture of the birth of a baby—presuming we knew the man's wife was expecting. We communicate with each other all the time through such gestures and objects even when we do not speak.

Observe, too, that communication includes much more than facts or knowledge. What we often communicate is ourselves, our present state, our values, our inner selves. For example, the new father isn't just sharing a fact with us, the birth of a baby girl. He's sharing his exuberance, his pride, his joy in parenting. He shares his "spirit" with us. If we are at all sensitive and open, we are caught up in, affected by that spirit. We feel more joyful, we catch something of the spirit of parenting or recall our own earlier experience of parenting.

All human communication, therefore, involves signs (words, gestures and objects that possess a commonly understood symbolic quality). All human communication implies a sharing of ourselves with others, a revelation through these signs and symbols of "who we are and what we stand for" at this particular moment. All human communication also implies an invitation to respond, to accept this revelation, to enter "communion" with the one communicating himself.

Obviously, there are many degrees to this kind of communication. A polite "good morning" accompanied by a nod is a form of communication but will not have the intensity or effect for communion that an intimate embrace and "I love you" has when two lovers meet. Deep communication always has something of the quality of encounter we spoke of earlier. That is the kind of communication we are most interested in since it is the kind of communication between ourselves and Jesus we hope to experience in the sacraments. But to experience real communication or encounter requires a general sensitivity, alertness and openness to the signs by which people communicate with us. It is always a two-way street. If we miss the signs people are using or if we resist the invitation contained in them, no real communion will take place.

In speaking of signs as the means by which people communicate, we must be careful to distinguish between effective signs and what might be called pointers. The latter are what we most often mean when speaking of a sign: Exit, Stop, Rest Room, First Aid. These words printed on doors or posts give us instructions, show the way to something else, but of themselves they are empty. They do not affect us.

Effective signs, on the other hand, always contain or possess or do what they signify. For example, we've all probably ignored a STOP sign at one time or another as when traveling on a country road with good visibility. The sign gave us an instruction but it didn't have within it any reality of "stopness." But the man giving us the cigar is an effective sign. The act contains a capacity, a reality of sharing in one's joy. It is not something we can simply ignore. It demands a response, even if it is a negative one. We cannot totally ignore it.

Similar effective signs surround us in our everyday lives. A handshake is a sign of friendship and the very act of shaking hands has the capacity of forming or deepening the friendship. In the same way the handshake that seals an agreement is a gesture that somehow does what it signifies. It is a sign that effects something. We can see this to some degree in the policeman's uniform. It's a sign. As a police officer, the very sight of his uniform in a potentially disorderly situation tends to affect the group and bring a settling influence to it.

In other words, an effective sign, as opposed to a pointing sign, somehow contains and does what it signifies. When we talk about people communicating through signs, we mean primarily through effective

signs. Our smile contains what it signifies—our plea-
sure, approval, appreciation, affection—and it affects
the recipient of our smile accordingly. Our gift of flowers contains our love, our gratitude, our apology and it
communicates *us* to the other. The act of receiving the
flowers is in fact the act of receiving us. It is in this act
of giving and receiving a sign that encounter and communion can be achieved.

While we are jumping ahead at this point, the relation of all this to the sacraments should be obvious. The
sacraments are signs by which Jesus communicates
with us. The signs used somehow contain and do what
they signify.

With this background in mind let us refocus on the
goal of this unit: to awaken or sensitize students to the
nature, role and effect human signs and symbols have
in our everyday life and in our communication with one
another.

I. *A Beginning*

A possible starting point would be to give each
student a slip of paper with a particular "I" statement
on it. A typical list would include some of the following:

I love dogs.
I apologize.
I love you.
I am a new father (mother).
I hate cats.
I am a famous rock and roll star.
I am a Christian.

I love horses.

I am proud to be an American.

I am proud to be Black (Indian, Mexican-American, etc.).

More than one person could be given the same "I" statement if working with a large group. Instruct each person to try to find a way through gestures, posture, facial expressions and any available objects to communicate his or her "I" statement to others. The only rule is that they cannot talk or otherwise use the words contained in their "I" statement. If they choose to write or draw something as part of their communication, it must be symbolic in nature, e.g., "I love dogs" could be expressed in part with the picture of a dog food.

This is usually more effective when some materials and objects are available to use as props or symbols for the project. After sufficient time, about five to ten minutes, each person attempts to communicate his "I" statement. Depending on the size of the class, this could be done in smaller groups of about six or eight. The students, of course, are to try and guess each other's "I" statement. When all have had the opportunity to communicate in this way, regroup the entire class and seek reactions to the activity.

Normally, questions like, "Who seemed cleverest or most humorous?" will get it started. Other questions like, "Did you find it difficult? Why?" serve well too. In younger groups especially, there are usually plenty of spontaneous reactions. The teacher's task is to guide discussion toward a reflection upon communication in general and the role of signs and symbols in our everyday communication. We are concerned too with why some signs seem more effective than others. In this context, distinction is made between effective signs and pointer signs. Try to use as examples some of the signs developed by the students in the exercise. Reference could/should be made to the sign of the cross, its meaning and its effect, as when making it in a public restaurant, in the midst of a sports event, in a small group before prayer, etc. What does it say about you, what are you trying to say when using it, what effect does it have—pro and con—on those around you? Similar questions could be asked of other common signs like a handshake or the gesture of giving a gift.

In short, the elements and nature of a sign as a normal means of communication should be explored. While the teacher may have to take some initiative here, as much as possible, students should be kept involved by offering personal examples. The next step will involve doing this same thing more systematically. The teacher need not try to exhaust all the concepts in one session. The main purpose of the activity and discussion is to begin to alert students to the presence of signs in their lives and to see how these signs work. Once that is done, they will be ready for the next step. However, there are some alternate approaches to beginning this unit.

New Handshake. In this activity, students are asked to comment about various popular handshakes now in vogue or similar kinds of greetings popular among young people. Then challenge them in pairs or small groups to attempt to devise a new handshake that is symbolic of a particular group's values:

football players' handshake
cheerleaders' handshake
hot rod driver/motorcycle enthusiasts' handshake
fishermen's handshake

bowlers' handshake
tennis players' handshake
meatcutters' handshake, etc.

The list is virtually endless and the exercise usually takes a humorous turn. Its purpose obviously is to lead into the whole question of the role of signs, the variety of signs (other than the handshake), the importance of signs on everyday communication as described above.

Advance Team. In this approach, the teacher would select a group of cooperative students well in advance of class and work with them to prepare several signs like those suggested above the "I" statements. Each person would present his or her sign to the entire class for them to guess its significance. The advantage here is that the teacher could help tailor the signs so they better exhibit the various qualities and kinds of signs used in our communication. In this way, less is left to chance and it is easier both to initiate and to guide the discussion along the desired lines. Its disadvantage is in reducing the majority of the class to spectators. To counter this, the teacher may invite each student to participate by making a sign once the idea has been demonstrated by the Advance Team.

II. *The Next Step*

Once the concept of sign has been introduced and students have some feel for it, the next step is to attempt to refine their understanding. This is often best done in two stages. First is what might be called a recognition exercise. Second is what might best be called a definition exercise.

In the first stage, the task is simply to ask students

to try to identify as many effective signs as they can think of that occur in their daily lives. For starters, the teacher might want to provide some obvious examples: handshake, gift giving, smiles. Students can do this best in groups, but each could be asked to do it privately and then share the list with others. A third alternative is for the whole class to do this together, using a blackboard or newsprint for recording what they "shout out."

Once a reasonable list is compiled, the task is to go through it to distinguish effective signs from pointer signs, since usually it will contain some of both. It is in this process that the teacher can help the students understand the distinction between the two. It also provides opportunities for the teacher to comment, clarify and question. In doing this, the test should always be: What does this particular sign *do*, or what is it intended to *do*?

In this same context the whole question of symbol and the symbolic should be raised and refined. Man makes symbols when he takes natural objects like a rock and gives them a particular significance like strength or permanence. Thus the Prudential Life Insurance Company attempts to communicate its reality through the use of symbol—the Rock of Gibraltar. While that symbol can also be used as a pointer saying this is a Prudential office, its primary function is to say something, to communicate one's reality, to instill confidence and consequently to invite communion.

Man can also take some words and give them a symbolic value. This is what we do when we create mottos or slogans. This is what happens when a word takes on deeper meanings because of circumstances as with the word "Watergate." It now refers to a whole complex of values or the lack of them and not just to a place or to a thing that lets water in and out.

Man can also invent symbols from his own imagination even though they have no exact duplicate in nature. The American Flag is a symbol and consequently has potential as an effective sign when used in particular ways. The design itself was "created."

In this same process of identifying and evaluating various signs, the teacher will want to return especially to the role of signs as communication between persons —as means by which people reveal themselves and invite others to communion. Thus tears can be a sign. So is an embrace, a kiss, a butt pat. The question asked about signs (What do they *do*?) could be restated: What is revealed and what kind of invitation is extended by one person to another?

The second stage of this process flows from the activity of identifying and evaluating various kinds of signs. It is to ask the students to attempt now to develop their own definition of what is meant by effective sign. This is best done in small groups since it provides a good opportunity for peers to help one another clarify their thinking. It also insures that the less articulate students will benefit by the exercise. Left alone they often feel quite inadequate.

The benefit of this activity should be obvious. It clarifies thinking and at the same time continues to heighten the students' sensitivity to the whole question of sign and communication in their daily lives.

The teacher's role is not so much to give the definition as it is to help students arrive at an acceptable one.

This second stage is important and should not be eliminated. However, there are some alternatives to the first stage, namely identifying signs.

Search for Signs Field Trip. Using the field trip principle, students would be asked to go to appropriate places such as shopping centers to see how many "signs" they can detect in operation there among the people. Some prior instruction is necessary here regarding the distinction between effective and pointer signs. Again, the school halls or cafeteria could be used for the project. Upon returning students would share what they saw, and from this a list could be developed as above for refining and clarifying purposes.

Film Viewing. Virtually any film will contain many signs of the type we are discussing. Often they now come through as clichés. Even the "white hat" the good guy wore in old westerns now has a kind of symbolic value. It is possible to alert students to signs by having them attempt to detect them in a film you choose to show. Some prior instruction about what to look for will be necessary.

Both these alternates could also be used as follow-up activities for the first exercise mentioned above.

III. *The Heart of the Matter*

By developing sessions and activities along the lines suggested so far, it is possible to sensitize students to the role of signs in human communication. Critical in all this, however, is the goal of communication, namely communion. Through signs we reveal something of ourselves and invite others to accept that which we reveal: our happiness, sorrow, friendship, displeasure, gratitude, help, etc.

So signs are a means to an end. They are ultimately intended to initiate, deepen and perfect human relationships. In the last analysis the relationship is what is desired.

This will have critical implications later for understanding and appreciating our whole sacramental system, so it becomes the central point in this unit.

Perhaps the most effective way to dramatize the effect of signs on human relationships is an activity like the following. After a brief explanation of how we reveal ourselves through signs for the purpose of forming (or destroying) human relationships, ask the students to help you test out this theory.

Explain that giving a gift, which will have already been discussed by now, is a generally understood sign in our culture. It reveals good will, friendship, appreciation and approval to another. The students' task is to see what happens when they offer gifts to total strangers as in a shopping center or a downtown street. The choice of the gift is important here. It should be something inexpensive but with a symbolic quality like a flower or smile buttons. Students can help determine the kind of gift suitable and possible.

The students' demeanor in offering the gift is also critical since (and you should stress this) it is part of the overall sign. For that reason they should try to avoid any behavior that would seem to indicate the offering is a joke or trick. It must be as sincere a gesture as possible. Also, it is best to do this activity alone or in small groups of two or three. Larger groups would arouse suspicion and make the experiment ineffective. A large group is itself a kind of sign and has effects on human relationships. All these points, of course, should be discussed with the students so they can decide the actual details of the experiment.

As soon as possible after the experiment, students should be assembled to discuss the results. What happened? Normally there is sufficient material for lively discussion and the teacher would want to give all students time to share whatever they felt was important. Normally, too, the experiences range from total rejection, even anger by some strangers to striking up a friendly relationship with them. Given these extremes and the variety of experiences in between, the teacher would want to help the students analyze the reasons for such variations. This leads to the important point that unless people are open and trusting, they will often reject signs of friendship even when sincerely offered. This openness or trust is often called—and legitimately —*faith*.

On the other hand, the quality of the sign is important. Some signs are more effective than others. Also the same sign could have different meanings for different people. In a high crime area, two youths standing together and approaching strangers could signal danger and not friendship.

As much as possible, such observations should be elicited from the students themselves, but to the degree necessary the teacher will want to guide the discussion in these directions. In the context of recent experience and new awareness of some of the elements of sign and communication, it is also good to ask them to look back now at some past experiences. Can they think of instances where they did make a sign of friendship (or any other kind of self-revelation and offering) and were rejected? Instances where they were on the receiving end and either misread or rejected the signs of another? Positive experiences where a relationship was deepened and where a particular sign played a key part? Why?

In any event the experience usually provides ample interest and a good teaching opportunity for stressing certain key points. In list form they include:

1. A sign usually consists of a variety of elements: words, gestures and objects. The overall situation also plays a part in the effectiveness of a sign—what it does to the other.
2. It is by signs that we reveal ourselves to others and invite them into relationship or communion. Signs are integral to all human community and communicators.
3. One's openness, sensitivity, trust, alertness are critical in all this—signs don't work when there is no *faith*.
4. Signs change us—demand either that we accept or reject the person "signing"—once we recognize the sign as such.

As an alternate or as a follow-up to the above, these activities might also be useful.

Going Home. After some initial discussion about the role of sign in forming or altering relationships, ask the students to perform an experiment at home. They are to decide on a sign (again stress the various elements: words, gestures, objects) intended to communicate their love, gratitude, apology or whatever is appropriate to some member of their family with whom they'd like to improve their relationship. To give them some ideas, suggest that it could be anything from a greeting card or flowers to cleaning up one's room *before* being asked.

At the next session ask for reports about what happened. While you can anticipate that some will have forgotten or just didn't do it, normally enough will have tried it to give a basis for the kind of discussion described above.

Ambassadors. If it is unrealistic to send a whole class out on the experiment, it can often be done effectively through a small group of volunteers. The class could help them decide the details of the experiment. They would carry it out and then report back to the class. Discussion is then initiated.

Also, it is sometimes helpful to have a small group carry out and report on the experiment first as a means of generating interest before sending the whole group out on their own experiment.

Summary

Through a series of sessions along the lines described above, it is usually possible to help students arrive at a greater awareness and understanding of the roles of signs in human relationships and the nature of human communication.

If time, interest or the caliber of the students makes it possible as a good context for spending a while exploring some of man's most creative symbolic expressions: fine art, music, poetry, drama, the dance, the whole role of these in forming and developing human community could be explored. Also it would be good, if possible, to allow students more time for expressing themselves symbolically. In this context activities like making collages, writing haikus, constructing banners and similar activities popular in religious education programs continue to have a role. They can sensitize students to the nature and function of the symbolic in their own lives. In any event, by the end of this unit the students should be ready for a more intelligent exploration into the role of ritual celebration in their lives and the role signs and symbols play in these ritual celebrations. That is our next task.

4. "Play It Again, Sam"

Introduction

The overall goal of this unit is to alert students to the role of ritual in their lives and to help them come to an understanding of the nature and purpose of ritual celebrations. Some background information might be useful here.

First we should distinguish between the popular meaning of the word ritual and its more technical meaning. We often say, "He goes through a regular ritual when he shaves each morning." Or, "I had to go through a regular ritual in order to get my driver's license renewed." When used in these ways, what we usually refer to is some very predictable, orderly, socially expected or relatively unchanging behavior. That is the popular meaning of ritual.

Used in a more technical sense, ritual is usually associated with celebration. In this sense a ritual is described as we have spoken of it earlier. It is a group's attempt to recall, re-enact, or re-present a significant event of the past by means of carefully chosen words, gestures, objects most suited to that purpose. Because these elements in the celebration have much symbolic value they are preserved and do not change too readily. Hence, ritual celebration.

The actual celebration has a purpose that looks to

the future as well as to the past. By recalling our past and celebrating it in the present, we give our lives new energy and direction for the future.

We can also distinguish between secular rituals, quasi-religious rituals and specifically religious rituals. A high school football banquet has all the elements of a ritual celebration in the secular sense. Its purpose is to recall the past season, all past moments of glory, its successes and its sorrows; to celebrate that past now through speeches, (most of these speeches are rather predictable in the ritual as well as in the rhetorical sense), the giving of awards, the display of trophies and the sharing of a meal (also rather predictable in terms of quality and menu). Some other symbols include the singing of the school song, the display of the school colors and the like. This banquet also projects us into the future with pledges and promises of future victories. Such banquets have a value to the persons involved for a variety of reasons and can correctly be called a ritual celebration.

Quasi-religious ritual celebrations would include the birthday party for most families as well as the family celebration of events like Thanksgiving and anniversaries. Usually, rather elaborate rituals develop in most families as they celebrate these events year after year.

Finally we have religious rituals. As we have seen, these are intended to celebrate religiously significant moments of our ancestors' past. In celebrating them we experience something of what they experienced. Clearly this is what we intend to do each time we celebrate any sacrament. It is especially true in our celebration of Eucharist.

Translated into topics for student study, our first

concern will be with helping them to discover the purpose of ritual and that it is integral to human life. It is not something "invented" only by religious people. In the process we will want to help them identify the elements of ritual celebration and finally will want to attempt to give them some experience of how ritual celebration can "make the past a present experience."

I. *A Beginning*

One of the best ways to introduce students to the topic of ritual celebration is to involve them in developing one. What follows is an example of how this can be done. Explain that the Senate has just commissioned them (the students) to develop a memorial celebration to be used on the 4th of July in all cities throughout the country. An unlimited budget is available. (If the group is large, it is best to divide the students into smaller groups of six to eight. Each group would have the same task.) Instructions given by the Senate include these:

1. Its primary purpose is to recall the key events and especially the key values involved when the nation first declared its independence and became a nation.
2. It should last no longer than one hour.
3. It should include appropriate signs and symbols.
   NB. Keep in mind that sign is used here in a broad sense to mean words, gestures, objects, setting, the participation of the people, etc.
4. The desired effect is that by "re-living" this historic event the participants will come away from the celebration with a sense of rededication to ideals of freedom.

Encourage the students to "think big" since money is no problem. You may want to give them some help in terms of suggesting possibilities, like the value of interpretive dance, the role of speeches in this kind of celebration, the effectiveness of a well produced "light-slide-film" show as part of the celebration.

At the same time remind the students that they should be prepared to explain and justify the particular signs and symbols they choose. What event or value do they represent? Does the sign or symbol chosen truly speak a common language? Will the people present recognize it?

Time for the activity will vary. Some students can get very involved in this type of thing. Others could find it very difficult. Normally about a half hour is sufficient. But if interest is good, a whole session could be spent on developing the celebration. In any event, when the groups have completed the project, ask them to share the results with the rest of the class. The various celebrations can be critiqued by the class as a whole. Will it work? Why? Why not? Did anything stand out as an especially good sign? Why? Were any common themes or signs running through all the celebrations?

In the context of analyzing these celebrations presented by the students the discussion should be moved to the concept of ritual celebration in general. Do we have many such celebrations in our regular life? Often students do not make the immediate connection so the teacher may want to suggest a specific one like the football banquet or the birthday party. What do the rituals just developed seem to have in common with all ritual celebrations? What seems to be the purpose behind all ritual celebrations? Can anyone tell us of a ritual celebration experienced that seemed particularly effective? What made it effective? What effect did it in fact have?

If the students do not arrive at the insight themselves, the teacher will want to introduce the idea that in addition to these secular or social ritual celebrations there is the whole area of religious ritual celebrations. But this should not be forced since as long as discussion of secular rituals is productive, the initial purpose is being served: alerting the students to the nature and role of ritual in their lives. A side activity that can flow directly from this discussion is to ask the students in groups to identify as many ritual celebrations as they can which they have experienced. In compiling and sharing these lists the teacher has an opportunity to see if the students are in fact understanding what is meant by ritual celebration. These are the key concepts one hopes the students will grasp:

1. Ritual celebrations are attempts to recall and to re-enact a past event.
2. The main means of doing this is through the use of effective signs and symbols, ones which in some way contain the values and make present those events of the past.
3. Signs and symbols should be understood in the broad sense as words, gestures, objects and the overall setting which includes the participating group.
4. An effective celebration is one that reminds us of the past event so vividly that we virtually "re-experience" it and consequently gain renewed dedication, motivation or enthusiasm.
5. At the same time an effective celebration depends on the openness, receptivity or "faith" of the participants.

Once the students have gained this kind of insight and are made more aware of the kinds of ritual celebrations they are experiencing in their everyday lives, we are ready to move on in depth to the question of religious celebrations. To get them to that point one of the following could also be used as an alternate or follow-up to the above activity.

Happy Birthday. This is basically a discussion type activity but because it is well within the experience of each student, it can be very effective. Simply ask the students in small groups to share with each other how their families celebrate birthdays. In the process ask them to give as many details as possible. Next ask them if any common elements can be identified—things that almost all families do in celebrating birthdays. Using these lists of common elements as the jumping off point, the teacher can then introduce the idea of ritual celebration and proceed as suggested above. With this kind of beginning it is often possible to introduce the Independence Day project as a follow-up. It will make more sense then and will create more interest among students.

The Real Thing. As an alternative to the "make-believe" project of Independence Day it would be ideal if the group had the opportunity to develop an actual ritual celebration. Occasions include the anniversary of a school or parish, a surprise birthday party for a teacher or one of the parish priests, a retirement or going-away party for some teacher or student, etc. One especially good occasion is to involve students in planning the parish's Thanksgiving Liturgy since this serves as a good bridge from ritual in general to religious ritual and sacrament. In the process of such actual planning there are ample opportunities for making the observations and explaining to the students the key concepts involved in ritual.

II. *The Next Step: Religious Ritual*

In one sense this step is optional since with the kind of background the students should have acquired by now, it is possible to move directly into the question of sacramental rituals. However, there is a value in taking an intermediate step if time allows. Basically it involves the experience of a religious ritual celebration other than Christian. Ideally suited for this would be a Seder Supper planned and celebrated by the class. In larger cities students will often have access to Buddhist temples where they could witness a ritual celebration. Another alternative would be to attend a liturgy of one of the Eastern Rites of the Catholic Church.

In lieu of the possibility of actually experiencing any of these, it might be possible at least to invite guest speakers representing particular non-Christian religions to explain their rituals to the students.

Another option would be to assign research projects to the students. The task would be to read about and then report about a ritual of one of the non-Christian religions either past or present. For example, certain Roman and Greek religious rituals are excellent for analyzing all the elements of ritual itself. In fact, various mystery religions of the first century have obvious parallels to the development of our own sacramental system. Such research would center on determining the original experience which is being re-enacted and the kinds of signs used for this re-enactment.

The purpose of pursuing any of these activities is

to deepen the students' appreciation of the role religious rituals have always played in human life. To put it another way, sacraments are not unique to Christians even though the Christian sacraments are unique. In our time many students are critical of the Church and feel certain aspects of Church life (e.g., the sacraments) are irrelevant. It is advisable to impress upon them the fact that religious ritual celebrations are indeed integral to human life. Man has always had such "sacraments."

It might be noted that this would not be a good time to analyze the way other Christian denominations celebrate sacraments. The reason for this is twofold. First, it could create confusion if students have not first studied in some depth the concept of Christian sacraments as such. Second, our major purpose is to help students to discover that religious ritual or sacrament is not unique to the Christian tradition but can be found in one form or other in virtually any religion.

III. *The Heart of the Matter*

In this unit the "heart of the matter" is actually moving into the topic of our own sacramental rituals. However, it is best once again to give the students an experience of developing a ritual rather than talking about it. For our purposes the following activity can be quite effective.

Tell the students you are asking them to make a "sacrament." The task will be similar to the activity of developing a patriotic ritual. However, this time what you are trying to recall and re-enact through well chosen signs and symbols is one of the events in Jesus' life. The teacher has two options here. One would be to identify the precise event in the Gospel. For example, the event of Jesus raising Lazarus from the dead. The other would be to allow the students to choose a Gospel event that interests them. In either case the event should be relatively concrete, like the multiplication of the loaves. This would be easier to ritualize than an event like the Transfiguration. Include in the instructions reminders about the variety of sign, how the setting and participation of the people are parts of the overall sign, how the ultimate purpose is to try to so vividly re-create the event that the participants obtain some experience of what the original event must have been like for those who witnessed it.

Unlike the patriotic ritual, in this activity the groups will be asked actually to perform the ritual. Therefore, it should be relatively short in length. Materials for making "signs" and actual objects for ritualizing (e.g., bread) would have to be provided. For this reason there normally should be a planning session during which the students develop the ritual and then a performance session. Between the two the students would have time to make or acquire the signs they had decided upon.

During the planning session the teacher would want to participate primarily as a consultant. It is time to ask questions about "why" that sign, what are you in fact trying to re-enact, what kind of values or experience are they trying to "make present." In this way the activity provides an excellent teaching opportunity because it focuses on such concrete, immediate matters.

Options include some of those mentioned in relation to other activities. The teacher might want to ask a group of volunteers to do this rather than involve the whole class. Or the ritual may have a real purpose such as becoming part of an actual celebration or prayer service within the parish on a particular feast day.

In this type of activity the students will often gravitate toward a very realistic representation, something along the order of a pageant. Encourage them, however, to move more in the direction of the symbolic. Also encourage them to build into the ritual some form of group involvement, even if it is no more than saying something together.

Given the nature of the event being ritualized, the actual atmosphere for the presentations should be as serious (as opposed to humorous) as possible. They should be approached with a more prayerful than theatrical attitude.

Once the rituals are celebrated (or as many as are judged suitable) students should be invited to critique them. Which ones seemed most effective and best put us "in touch" with the event? Why? What signs seemed especially effective? Why?

From this kind of critiquing the teacher will want to move the discussion into a new direction by asking something like this: If we say people "get in touch" with each other through signs, is it possible for us to "get in touch with Jesus" through signs specially chosen because they are expressive of him, his actions and his values?

A kind of follow-up to that question would be: What is the difference between these rituals we have just developed and the seven sacraments of the Church?

Note, we have finally moved to the real issues, but hopefully by now the students will have had enough background and experiences to begin to wrestle with the questions just introduced. Depending on the quality of the responses the students make to these questions (it is often effective to present these questions to students in groups, allowing them to work out a group answer rather than individual answers) the teacher will take a more or less active part in providing the answers.

In any event, it is at this point that an actual definition of the sacraments should be developed and considered by the students. The key elements of this definition would include:

1. A sacrament is a ritual celebration of particular events/actions in Jesus' life.
2. This ritual representation is provided primarily through signs that communicate something of the person, actions and values of Jesus.
3. These ritual representations actually become situations or events through which Jesus is in fact present to us and communicates himself to us.

One alternate for developing this kind of definition is for the teacher to provide several statements of the kind just offered and ask students to evaluate and react to them in groups: agree? disagree? why? what would you change?

The time spent in developing and analyzing the nature of the sacraments will vary depending on the resistance, misunderstanding or agreement found within the class. In any case, this session or series of sessions should be viewed by the teacher as basically an introduction. The units that follow will attempt to develop these key ideas in more detail. The goal to be reached before moving on to the next unit is primarily to bridge the gap between all the past ideas that have been developed and the *question* of the nature of our sacraments. In other words, once the question is understood in relationship to all the past experiences related to signs, communication and ritual, we are ready to discuss the question directly. While there must be alternatives to this activity of developing a ritual related to a Gospel event, I honestly do not know of any more effective ones for our purposes. The one option would be to eliminate the process of actually celebrating the rituals. Once developed "on paper" they could serve as an adequate base for raising the question. However, the experience is always to be preferred.

Summary

It may seem to have been a circuitous route to opening a discussion on the nature and purpose of the Church's sacraments. Yet, if the teacher has the time and patience to go through the various steps—or at least those most needed by the students—the end result will be worth it. The students will normally display an openness to the question and will have enough personal background to enter into the following sessions intelligently. If we keep in mind the fact that our long range goal is to introduce them into a life style and not just impart certain facts, this gradual, experience-oriented process will make sense.

We are now ready to *teach* the sacraments themselves.

5. "Do This in Memory of Me"

Introduction

This will be a busy unit. First, we will be involved in the whole question of faith as it relates to the sacraments. Second, we will want to experience an actual sacramental celebration, a Eucharist, in the light of this understanding of the role of faith. Finally, we will want to analyze that celebration in some detail in order to identify the essential elements of any sacrament.

As background we should recall that openness, sensitivity or faith is necessary if we are to be able to recognize what is happening around us. It is also necessary to recognize what people are in fact revealing to us through signs. This is especially true in the case of the sacraments since Jesus' presence is revealed and his action is experienced through the signs the Church uses to celebrate a sacrament. Without faith we do not "see Jesus" present and acting. In terms of the sacraments we must reverse the old adage "seeing is believing" and say "believing is seeing."

Obviously this faith is not quite the same as the power of suggestion, as in the trick where we can convince a person one piece of rope is longer than another through group pressure. In fact, there is really no similarity between that psychological trick and faith. In religious faith, the faith required in the sacraments, we are dealing with a more fundamental and relatively stable mind set. It is even more than a mind set. It is a relationship.

Faith is analogous to that bond between husband and wife, between mother and child, between two friends. It is an attitude of total acceptance and total surrender. It is an openness and sensitivity to the other based on this total acceptance (love is a synonym for faith) which allows the wife to read volumes in a single glance (sign) of the husband and which allows the mother to be alert and to interpret every whimper, sigh and smile (all are signs) of the infant.

The key issue here, of course, is that the celebration of the sacraments does not create this faith. Rather it is the faith brought to the sacraments that makes them "happen." In other words, unless a person has a basic attitude of friendship, love or acceptance of Jesus before celebrating a sacrament, he will not recognize Jesus under the signs of the sacrament. On the other hand, if a person comes with such a basic attitude, it is strengthened by the very contact with Jesus through the sacrament.

We must remember here that we are always talking about degrees of faith, not the perfection of faith. We can distinguish between three kinds of people: those who approach the Eucharist with no faith, those who come with some minimal faith and those who come with a very profound faith. (All shades of degree in between are also possible.) The Eucharist will obviously have a different effect on each of the three. The first will "see" nothing. The second will "see" something, but will not be too moved. The third will "see" all kinds of things and go away profoundly moved.

The film, "The Eye of the Beholder," very popular

in religion classes a few years ago is a good illustration of this point. This point, incidentally, is precisely what we need to stress to the students. Sacraments are not magic. What you "see" is what you get and what you "see" depends on the faith you bring to the celebration.

This now becomes a critical moment in the whole process of our sacraments program. It would be useless to go on seeking the more sophisticated appreciation of sacraments toward which we are striving if the students do not have a strong faith, or as is more common, they really do not understand the nature of faith.

To put it another way, sacraments are basically for the believer. This is even true of Baptism, since at least for the adult Baptism is received after a conscious conversion and a rather detailed program of instruction. Baptism is a celebration "after the fact" of becoming a believer and not the "cause" of belief. For that reason, it becomes necessary to challenge the students on the whole question of their faith in the reality of Jesus, his Sonship, his redemptive death and resurrection, his capacity to be present in the signs of the sacraments. It is also only fair to stress to them that it is their own personal faith which will make the sacraments "happen" for them. Their faith need not be perfect, but it must be. The sacraments aren't magic, faith-producing machines. They are an encounter with a person. We encounter a person only to the degree that we are open, sensitive, alert, *believing*.

The implication here should be obvious but we will spell it out anyway in case we have failed to state it clearly enough. Once we raise the question of faith in relation to the sacraments, it is possible that the whole program will take a different tack for the teacher. He or she *may* find it necessary to spend a great deal of time on the question of faith itself. It will not always be necessary, but it *may* happen. In that event it would be a futile academic exercise to continue to pursue the nature of sacraments as such. The more fundamental issue of "Who do you say I am?" would have to be pursued.

Presuming we can leap this very real hurdle, the next step will be to provide a Eucharist for the students. We will explore the implications of that now.

Having experienced a Eucharist the task involves exploring the essential elements of a sacramental celebration. These can be broken down into three categories: Before, During, After.

1. *Before*. A Sacrament begins *before* we gather to ritually celebrate it. This can be seen most easily in regard to the sacrament of marriage. Long before two people celebrate Matrimony, the marriage has begun. That is, the love relationship has begun to form. In fact, it has formed to such a degree that the couple are willing to make a public profession that, with the help of Jesus, it will last forever. Jesus has already "been involved" during the development of this love relationship. That is, Jesus has been important to the couple. So to celebrate Matrimony is in a real sense to ratify, to make public, to intensify a relationship with each other and with Jesus that has already begun to take shape.

We can also see this in terms of the Sacrament of Forgiveness. The sinner has already experienced a conversion before he approaches the sacrament. He is sorry for what he has done, intends to change his ways and reforms his relationship with God. In the sacrament itself all this is celebrated. The result is that his previous conversion is publicly ratified and intensified through the sacramental encounter with Jesus. One could ask in this regard: "Why is it necessary to celebrate a sacrament such as marriage if in a real sense the marriage has already taken place before the ceremony?" The reason is twofold. On the one hand, being communal creatures or social animals there is a real need to "go public," to let people know who we are and what we stand for in order to be able to function within a community. This is true especially when our private convictions have a direct effect on the community. The community has a right to know certain things about us. Going public has a good effect on the community.

It also has a good effect on us. It affirms, strengthens, and intensifies our personal convictions. It makes us more responsible for them and less likely to change our minds about them. This is especially true in terms of the sacraments, since in their very celebration we encounter Jesus who enters into our lives as one who shares and supports the personal values being expressed in the celebration.

Not to act publicly is in a real sense not to act. Not to publicly celebrate our relationship to each other and to Jesus as signified in the Sacrament of Matrimony is to endanger if not destroy that relationship.

It is especially important to keep in mind that something must have been going on in our own lives before we gather to celebrate a sacrament. Unless, for example, our lives have been at least to some degree, lives of sharing and caring, there is nothing to celebrate when we gather for Eucharist. The Eucharist is not just a celebration of past events in Jesus' life. It is also a celebration of our own personal past and particularly the immediate past. If that past has been basically selfish, we will have a hard time entering into a celebration of Jesus' selflessness. We can also see that unless we have already begun to experience sorrow and conversion for our sinfulness, it is doubtful that we would even make the effort to approach the Sacrament of Forgiveness. We would have nothing to celebrate since the sacrament is a celebration of God's loving forgiveness in our regard, a forgiveness we have already begun to experience.

This is true of all the sacraments. Each begins in our personal lives. Our experience of Jesus' presence and love in our daily life becomes the foundation for our ritual celebration of events in Jesus' life. It is in the celebration that our own life and Jesus' life are united and harmonized in a new, more intense way. If Jesus is not present in our personal life, it is doubtful if we will recognize him under the signs of the sacraments.

2. *During.* Here we are concerned with the actual elements of the ritual celebration. These elements are various signs which when taken together form the basis for recalling and re-presenting particular actions of Jesus. Taken together, these same signs become the means by which we encounter or experience Jesus present and acting in our midst once again. They fall into several categories:

A. Words—This includes any required Scripture passages, prayers, communal responses, and homily or exhortation the Church has judged integral to the celebration.
B. Gestures or Actions—This includes any required action on the part of the minister and/or the community. E.G., the pouring of water, the anointing with oil, the receiving of the consecrated bread.
C. Objects—This includes any required objects, such as the water, oil, bread, salt, etc.

D. Minister—This refers to the person designated by the Church who has the responsibility for calling the people together and for directing the celebration. For example, in Matrimony it is actually the couple who perform these functions. The priest in this instance is a witness and official representative of the community.

E. Community—Every sacrament is by nature a communal celebration and for that reason the community must be present or at least represented.

In each of these categories we can distinguish between what is essential or necessary, what is normally required but can be eliminated for a good reason, and what is not required but can be added. For example, we can have a Eucharist without the reading of the Gospel, which is normally required, but we could not have a Eucharist without the words of consecration. We can have a Eucharist without candles and vestments, objects normally required, but we could not have a Eucharist without bread and wine.

Several things are important here. First, a sacrament is a combination of individual signs. It is the celebration taken as a whole that is important. It is the total experience which is the means through which we encounter Jesus. Second, we should not become careless about what is normally required in the ritual. For example, we should not eliminate a Gospel reading at the Eucharist without a good reason. At the same time we should not become so preoccupied with individual elements that we fail to recognize the total sign. For example, to become preoccupied with the question of unleavened vs. leavened bread is to miss the point that it is the act of sharing the consecrated bread in whatever form it appears that is the central sign. In short there is need for some restraint and some freedom in approaching individual elements that are *not absolutely essential* to the overall sign.

The role of the community as integral to the overall sign cannot be stressed too much. Everything about the community is important—its attitude, its participation, its position and posture are all elements that have a real influence on the overall celebration. Even what happens in the parking lot before Mass, for example, will have some effect on the community's ability to be a sign of love and unity at the Eucharist.

In the area of the non-essential but helpful, we include elements like the setting, decorations, the kind and quality of the music and whatever else contributes to the overall celebration. For example, a Baptism celebrated in a small crowded baptistry on a Sunday afternoon will be a different experience than one celebrated in the midst of the community during the Easter Vigil. Both are valid, of course, but the latter is likely to be more *significant* to all involved.

3. *After*. Just as a sacrament begins prior to the celebration, so it continues afterward. On the one hand, there is the personal experience one takes from the sacramental celebration: new awareness, dedication, motivation. We live more sacramental lives because of the sacrament. On the other hand, the community as a whole becomes more sacramental. For example, after witnessing a marriage celebration, the community itself shares some responsibility for helping the couple "make it work." The community will, from time to time, have to support, encourage or challenge the couple in order to help them live out their relationship to each other and to Jesus. The community must be a continuing sign of Jesus' involvement and concern in their marriage relationship. This is especially true in the case of infant

baptism. In a real sense the infant's faith is held in trust by the community until he or she is old enough to respond personally. The community has the role of being a continuing sign of Jesus' presence and acceptance to the developing child, a kind of continuing baptismal experience.

If we keep in mind the fact that the grace received in any sacrament is the gift of Jesus' presence, we can see better how the sacrament can be said to continue after the celebration and especially how it can continue through the community's relationship to the individual with its responsibility to be sacramental to others. Each of us can be a means for others to encounter Jesus' continuing presence in our midst.

Having reviewed some of the basic concepts about the role of faith and the nature of sacrament which we hope to impart to the students, we must now explore how we can best go about the task.

I. *A Beginning*

The concern here is to give the students some feel for the role faith plays in the celebration of sacraments. This activity is low key but can serve to initiate the desired discussion. Obtain a variety of pictures or objects related to various religions. A sample list might include a copy of the Old Testament, a picture of a Brahma bull, a picture of a Moslem mosque, a small statue or a picture of some Greek god. With each item an appropriate list of persons should be drawn up. Some examples could be:

Object: picture of a mosque
List of persons: an architect, an artist, an Israeli patriot, and a Moslem

Object: Old Testament
List of persons: a historian, a professor of Eastern
    Literature, a bookbinder and a devout Jew

Object: statue of Buddha
List of persons: a sculptor, a geologist, art collector
    and a devout Buddhist

Object: altar bread
List of persons: a baker, a Moslem, a Jew, a Bud-
    dhist, a devout Catholic

The number of objects and lists is optional but
usually about four or five are sufficient. The process is
to hold up the object or picture and then read the list of
persons. Ask the students to state how they think each
person on the list would view the object. Then ask why
each would probably view it differently. The last item
displayed should be the altar bread. Ask how each person would view *this during a Eucharist*. Why?

In each case, of course, it is faith that makes the
difference and in the last instance it is faith in Jesus.
This enables the teacher to initiate a discussion first of
all on the overall question of the nature of faith. We
can, for example, describe the Moslem, the Jew and
Buddhist as a believer just as much as we can describe
the Catholic as a believer. What are the common elements in the faith of each? What really is faith when
viewed in this general or generic sense?

If students do not arrive at it themselves, the
teacher will want to distinguish between faith as acceptance of truths and as a living, dynamic relationship.
Christian faith is above all a relationship with Jesus and
his Father. It is because of the relationship that we have
a kind of sensitivity or alertness or "eyes" for recogniz-

ing Jesus' presence in our lives and especially in the sacraments.

Once the topic of faith in relation to sacraments is raised, the teacher will want to ask the students their opinion of the role of faith in celebrating sacraments. Will anything happen if they approach the celebration without faith? with minimal faith? with very active, energetic faith?

Is this "auto suggestion"? What is the difference between faith and this kind of self-induced or group induced imagination—such as takes place in fake seances?

From here the teacher will want to raise more personal questions, such as: How real is Jesus to you? Who is he? What part does he play in your life just now? Do you really believe he becomes present to us in sacraments? These questions could be presented as rhetorical questions to stimulate self-questioning. In the right situation they could be presented as questions to be discussed together.

As mentioned in the Introduction the teacher should be in no hurry to move from this topic once the basic questions are raised. It may be necessary to spend several sessions on the whole question of faith in general, the students' personal experience of faith and the absolute necessity for faith in order to participate authentically in sacramental celebrations.

As an alternative for initiating this same kind of discussion, the teacher might consider the following activity called "Mock Pizza." This activity requires a little more involvement on the part of the teacher in that he or she must be both willing and able to provide a party for the class. Prior to the session prepare pieces of cardboard cut in the form of circles—one for each student. On each circle write a student's name and the word pizza. Prior to class advise two or three students that you are planning a little pizza party for the class. They are not to tell anyone, however, and during class they are to remain silent until called upon by you.

At the beginning of class hand out the pizzas to the students with no prior comments. Wait a moment for spontaneous reactions among them. Then ask the group as a whole what they see? Next ask them to look again, this time keeping in mind the previous activities related to sign. Now what do they see? Some may begin to get the point and guess that you are trying to tell them something or that the pizzas represent something you are going to do. At this point, ask the pre-advised students for their own reactions? What did they see? Why? Did the piece of cardboard signify a real pizza for them? What enabled them to "see" it? Ultimately what enabled them to see the cardboard pizza as a "real" pizza was not just their foreknowledge, but their "faith" in you, their overall relationship which told them you would keep your word to them.

This provides a good beginning for the above mentioned discussion on the whole question of faith and its relation to the sacraments. It also obviously demands that the teacher keep his word and at some point either during this class or in a future class provide a small party. Pizza is used here as an example. Any other appropriate word could be substituted to signify the kind of party promised.

II. *The Next Step*

The goal here is to provide a meaningful Eucharistic celebration. As preparation the teacher will want to review with the students some of the key ideas up to now: the nature of signs, the nature of ritual celebrations and the role of signs in these, and finally the role of faith in religious ritual celebrations. In the context of this kind of review the teacher can easily suggest that the group plan and celebrate a Eucharist together for the precise purpose of discovering if the experience will now make more sense to them than it may have done in the past.

The actual details of the celebration will depend on each teaching situation. No outline will be presented here. However, a few guidelines might be helpful.

First, it is very helpful for the dominant theme of the liturgy to center around the notion of faith. For example, the Gospel reading which relates the experience of the disciples on the way to Emmaus is ideal for our overall purposes.

Second, it should be kept relatively simple so as not to distract from the three main elements: the Liturgy of the Word, the Eucharistic Prayer itself, and the Communion. It would not be a good time, for example, to use a slide homily or introduce new songs.

Third, it is a good idea not to overexpose in terms of having the students too involved in the planning. All the elements would become too familiar and lose their intended sign value. It should have a certain freshness or "surprise" dimension to it for all the students.

Fourth, if the teacher will not be the celebrant, he or she must advise the priest ahead of time of what has been happening and why this Eucharist should have a special character to it. It would be disastrous for the celebrant to approach this Eucharist in a routine or perfunctory fashion.

By following these guidelines and the general principles for preparing and celebrating any liturgy in a meaningful manner, the overall experience for both teacher and students should be refreshing.

Following the liturgy there should be no formal activity or discussion. That will come in another session with the students. It is enough here to celebrate the liturgy and perhaps follow it with soft drinks and snacks (or have the pizza you promised).

III. *The Heart of the Matter*

As a follow-up to the Eucharist this session should be used to analyze what took place and to share what was experienced. To do this, the following form could be provided for each student:

Before	*During*	*After*
	1. Word	
	2. Action	
	a. of minister	
	b. of community	
	3. Object	

	Nothing					Very meaningful			
Overall Experience:	1 2 3	4	5	6	7	8 9 10			

Having given out these forms, the teacher should then take this opportunity to provide a straightforward explanation of the elements that go into making any sacrament. Included in the explanation should be the before, during, and after dimensions of any sacramental celebration. Distinction should be made between essential elements, required elements and optional elements. The overall combination of these provides the opportunity for encounter. With this kind of introductory explanation ask the students singly or in groups to attempt to identify any elements related to their particular Eucharist—before, during and after—which made a significant impression on them. These should be listed under the appropriate title. It is good to clarify that Word here refers to general categories of word signs rather than specific "words." For example, the homily is a word sign, the words of consecration are a word sign, the prayers of petition is a word sign. Also, they should rate the overall experience. After sufficient time, the lists should be shared and compared.

In the context of sharing and comparing, the teacher will have an opportunity for additional comments, clarifications and questions. By the end of the session you will normally have been able to present and explain in some detail tne entire structure or nature of a sacramental ritual. It will usually happen that some people will have a hard time identifying elements as particularly significant. Even this can work to the teacher's advantage. It will be necessary to find out why a homily that had a good effect on one person did not affect another or why the overall combination of signs provided a very real encounter experience for some and not for others.

There is one danger here. This is a time when the teacher is obviously leading and is also looking for "answers." Students will often revert to form and provide the answers the teacher wants, even if they are not how the student actually "saw" it. It is good to tell the students ahead of time that there are no "wrong answers" in this situation since what you are seeking is not theology but a description of their own experience. If they experienced nothing, they should so record it. This is especially important in their rating the "Overall Experience." If the activity is done in groups, this same problem arises in the form of group pressure. Therefore, each group should be allowed to provide a minority report.

In any event, the time has come for providing the students with some specific information about how the Church understands and celebrates sacraments. Hopefully, all the previous experiences have set a climate and prepared a receptivity for making this both possible and fruitful. For that reason, the following option to the above will in many instances be the more functional, especially with older and more sophisticated students.

Say It. Simply provide the students with a detailed outline of the key concepts presented in the background material above and speak directly to each item as it relates to their recent experience of the Eucharistic celebration. Following teacher input, allow time for group discussion and/or personal reaction. If the earlier experiences went well and the Eucharist was "good," we can skip the games and get into the real issues. In fact, this principle holds true throughout the program. Never "play a game" if the students already have enough experience upon which to reflect and the desire to do so.

Cross Section. One other alternative does work well in some situations. Talk with the students after the Eucharist (as many as possible) to get their immediate reactions. From the class select three or four, according to their reaction and their ability to share, and ask them to prepare a presentation for the class following the form given above. Ideally, the experiences should range from very turned on to blah. So choose at least one student who found the liturgy very meaningful and at least one who found it rather meaningless. Others could fall between the extremes.

After this presentation by the cross section, ask all the students to fill out a form for themselves. Then proceed as described above using the opportunities for clarifying and explaining as they occur.

Summary

Since the content of this unit is central to the whole program, the teacher should be willing to spend as much time as is needed on it. One word of caution, however: we do not want to over-analyze to the point where the sacraments are viewed too mechanically. There is an element of mystery here that we will never be able to fathom. What has been presented is a logical explanation, a way of coming to grips with the mystery. But the explanation will never dissolve the mystery. We should be careful to advise the students of this.

At the same time we must not over-emphasize the point that we experience Jesus in the sacraments. This could lead students to expect every liturgy to be a kind of an emotional trip, a spiritual "high," as it were. In stressing the reality of Jesus' presence in the celebration of sacraments, also stress that there will always be degrees to the actual experience of his presence. We do not want to give the students the idea that sacraments are a kind of Catholic seance wherein we conjure up a sensible presence. Our faith tells us he is present to us even when our senses or emotions remain unaffected by that presence.

In short, because we are now involved with the central concepts related to sacramental theology we must be cautious not to oversimplify. There must be a studied balance to the presentation to ensure that we do not leave the students with a distorted notion of sacraments.

Once the students achieve a basic understanding of the elements in the ritual celebration of our sacraments and have a reasonable expectation of what happens to them when they celebrate sacraments, we can move on to some other related questions. Specifically, we will examine the question of grace and its effects upon us. Then we will consider the history of the development of the seven sacraments and the particular grace each offers.

6. Grace Is More Than a Girl's Name

Introduction

The main concern in this unit will be grace. First, some background. Do you recall the Baltimore Catechism's definition of sacrament? "An outward sign instituted by Christ to give grace." We spent considerable time in earlier units re-examining what "outward sign" means. We have also re-examined what "instituted by Christ" means. In both instances we have attempted to expand the former rather literal interpretation of those phrases. In the past a too literal interpretation of "sign" for example, led to overemphasis of specific aspects of the ritual celebration. We got lost in details. A too literal interpretation of "instituted by Christ" led to endless debate about the precise text in the Gospels that marked the institution of a particular sacrament. The approach was narrow and distracted us from the deeper reality of sacraments. In the same way a too literal interpretation of "grace" has led us very often to understand the term as some "thing" that can be gained, stored up for lean times, or lost like water spilling through a cracked jar.

It is more common now to understand grace not as a thing but as God's presence or relationship to us; his offer of his friendship and his help, the sharing of his

Spirit with us. The word itself comes from the Latin, *gratia*, and means gift. The gift in this case is not a thing but a relationship, God's freely offered friendship.

In this sense any friendship is a grace because it always implies that one person freely offers himself to another. We cannot buy or earn a person's love. It must always be freely given. In the same way God's love for us is a gift, a divine grace, unearned and freely offered.

This is what is taking place in the celebration of any sacrament. Through the signs used by the Church Jesus becomes present to us precisely as a friend, offering us his love and his strength. Quite literally he is offering us the very Spirit by which he and the Father live.

You cannot store up a friendship. You can strengthen, maintain or destroy it. To return frequently to the Sacrament of Eucharist is to strengthen our friendship with Jesus. To lose grace is actually to reject the friendship, to break it off by betraying or rejecting the friend. To approach the Sacrament of Forgiveness is to restore the friendship, to offer the necessary apologies, make the necessary promises, receive the forgiveness that restores the friendship. It is to regain grace.

By describing a sacrament as a guaranteed opportunity to encounter Jesus, we describe it as a guaranteed opportunity for grace since it is a guaranteed opportunity to meet Jesus offering us his friendship and the strength it brings.

But we must recall that while the opportunity is guaranteed, there is no guarantee we will use it. We must keep in mind that sacraments do not work magic. Our free will is left intact. We must be open. We must be willing to receive Jesus offering himself to us through the signs of a sacrament. We have already seen this above when we stressed that we must bring faith to the sacrament.

The main point here, though, remains the nature of grace itself. By describing it as Jesus' presence and his freely offered friendship we are describing grace as a dynamic, intangible, unmeasurable reality. Grace is not quantitative. We cannot gain six points of friendship or lose six points of friendship. We describe friendship as strong or weak, unwavering or wavering, intense or indifferent. We describe it in qualitative terms. Being "in grace" is a way of living in relationship to God. It is not points, good marks or merits.

From God's point of view, then, grace is his offer of friendship. From our point of view grace is accepting and living in that friendship. From God's point of view grace is constant. He is always offering his friendship to us. From our point of view this relationship can grow stronger and deeper. It can become cold and can even be broken off. We can change our attitude toward God even if he does not change his attitude toward us.

We say this grace gives us strength. This, too, could be misleading and bring us back to a quantitative approach to sacraments. Strength here should be understood more in terms of the effect any friendship has on us. Through friendship we come under the influence of our friend. We view things from his point of view, are open to his suggestions; we judge things differently and consequently act differently because of our friend's influence over us, an influence we freely allow him to exercise.

To say grace gives us strength actually means that we are brought under the influence of Jesus. We are literally inspired by him. We live under the influence of his Spirit. The result is that we see things differently and we act differently. The deeper the friendship, the greater is Jesus' influence over us, the more "strength" we have to live according to his ideals or values. So we do not approach Confirmation or Eucharist or Penance to gain strength in the quantitative sense. We approach any sacrament in order to deepen our friendship with Jesus and allow ourselves to be brought more and more under the influence of his Spirit.

In this same context we can better understand the concept that each sacrament provides its own special kind of grace. Each ritual sacrament recalls and re-presents particular actions in the life of Jesus. These actions are indicative of particular values held by Jesus, his particular attitude toward certain human situations common to all men. The unifying theme of all these values is Jesus' desire for all men to form a community of peace and justice with each other and with the Father. So each sacrament is a particular act of "being community."

For example, Baptism reflects the process of being born into community, of being received and nurtured by the community, the necessary first step for each individual if there is ever to be community. At the other end of the human situation is the reality of sickness and death. The Sacrament of the Sick reflects the responsibility of the community to care for the sick in their midst and to support them in their final passage from the community. Between those extremes of entering the community at birth and leaving it at death are other key events integral to all human community. Coming of age, that is, assuming adult responsibilities within the community; marriage, the birth and rearing of children, which is essential to the continuation of community; identifying certain persons for special roles of service to the community; reconciliation for persons who have withdrawn from or become disruptive of harmonious communal life; and finally the day to day sharing of the life sustaining goods necessary for all community, symbolized in the daily meal, and symbolic of the sharing of all the fruits of human industry within community. For that reason the meal is symbolic of human community itself; it is both a means and the end of community. The sacramental equivalents of each of these integral elements in all human community is obvious. Each sacrament recalls and re-presents particular words and actions of Jesus working to establish and sustain human community in one or other of its dimensions.

For that reason we say in each sacrament Jesus is present to us offering his friendship and strength in a particular way. He is present to the marrying couple precisely to support them in the new life they are entering together, to be with them as a friend throughout that life with all its joys and trials. Jesus is present in the Sacrament of the Sick precisely as healing, supporting friend of the sick, helping them regain health, endure sickness and when necessary accept death.

To say that each sacrament gives a particular grace is to say that in each sacrament Jesus is present, offering us a particular dimension of his friendship. He offers us a particular kind of strength. He influences us in a particular way so that we can become or continue to be community to each other.

Eucharist, of course, is central to all the sacraments. First, it re-presents Jesus' death and resurrection in our behalf, which is the act that has made it possible for man to become once again a community gathered around one Father. Second, the symbolic nature of meal summarizes all that goes into being community—the day to day forgiving, working, sharing all things together. Jesus is present to us in Eucharist in this kind of universal way, as a friend in the total sense, offering to us every kind of strength we need to be community. In a real sense all the other sacraments lead to and flow from Eucharist. In a real sense the particular grace of each sacrament can be found in Eucharist. That is why we cannot celebrate Eucharist too often. That is why it is at Eucharist that we receive the "particular" grace to be Church. It is at Eucharist that we are most authentically Church. We also fulfill our mission as Church most completely by celebrating Eucharist.

It is obvious in Eucharist that the entire community receives a particular grace, the grace to be community. The other sacraments, however, could be misunderstood as personal, almost private matters if we misunderstand the overall nature of sacrament. Jesus is present both through and to the entire community in a particular way at each sacramental celebration. For example, at the celebration of a marriage, Jesus is present not just to the marrying couple but to the entire community as a friend, affirming and supporting the very institution of marriage. The entire community receives this particular grace of Jesus' presence. Its effect is to involve the whole community in the marriage of the couple, to influence them to support and encourage the couple in a continuing way and to uphold the institution of marriage.

In other words, when we are present at any sacrament we can never be spectators. We are part of the sign through which Jesus becomes present and to the degree that we are open we receive the particular grace of that sacrament even if we are not the ones "receiv-ing" it. To be present at a sacrament (meaning to be there as a faith-filled, attentive, receptive person) is to "receive" it. To "receive" any sacrament means pri-marily to encounter Jesus present and acting in the par-ticular way signified by the sacrament.

For example, to be present at any anointing even though not anointed is to experience Jesus present and actively concerned with the sick person. We are in-fluenced by Jesus' presence and his activity. We are drawn into it. While we are not the one being cared for, we are drawn into the act of caring. That is particular grace.

This was not stressed in sacramental theology dur-ing the period in the Church's recent past when so much emphasis was placed on private spirituality. Sac-raments were viewed as very individual, almost private matters. Today, however, with the re-emphasis on the communal nature of all sacraments, we are rediscover-ing that to be present at any sacrament is in a real sense to receive it and its particular grace.

Three summary concepts embrace what we have been saying about grace:

1. The grace of the sacrament is the gift of Jesus' pres-ence, the offer of his friendship and the sharing of his Spirit.
2. Particular grace of any sacrament refers to that aspect of communal life Jesus is strengthening by his presence and offering in his friendship. It is what Jesus is doing for us in a particular sacrament.
3. Every sacrament is communal in nature. The sacra-ments are intended to strengthen community; the whole community receives the sacrament's particular grace.

I. *A Beginning*

As a means of introducing the concept of grace as a relationship rather than a thing, the following activity can be useful. Some preliminary arrangements are necessary. You will need several decks of playing cards, some scotch tape, a mitten or sock for each student, and one cigar or similar size box for each group.

Divide students into at least two groups. If the class is large you may wish to form several groups. Explain the task in this way:

1. Each group is to try to pick up all of the cards in a deck scattered on the floor in their midst and place the cards in the box provided. Each group will work against time, trying to beat the other group(s).
2. Each person puts the sock or mitten on one hand. The other hand must be kept behind the back at all times.
3. Each person in Group A will be provided with a small piece of scotch tape which can be used to help pick up the cards. Persons are not to assist each other.
4. Group B will have one person who will have an uncovered hand. With that hand he is allowed to lift the cards up so others in the group can grasp them but he must keep one corner of the card on the floor until someone grasps it.
5. The object is to see which of the two is most advantageous.
N.B. If there are more than two groups, several can be designated A and several can be designated B.

Arrange the groups in circles and scatter a deck of cards in the midst of each group. They begin at your signal. Scoring can be done by waiting until a group picks up all the cards. That group is the "winner." Or you can set a time limit and count the cards in each box when the time is expired.

When the game is over, gather the groups together and ask their observations with some of the following questions: Which group seemed to have the advantage? Why? Was any kind of cooperative spirit developed with the group using scotch tape? In the group with the "free agent"? How did those using tape feel toward the others in their group? How did those with the "free agent" feel toward one another? Toward the free agent? Why?

After obtaining their initial observations switch to a more direct form of questioning with some of the following: Which of these group arrangements (A or B) in your opinion most reflects "how the grace of sacraments work"? Why?

Note: This will usually stop them, at least temporarily. For that reason it is often effective to re-form the groups at this point and ask each group to discuss the question among themselves for about five - ten minutes to try to come up with a good answer. Do not give any more clues. Allow them to struggle with it. After sufficient time, solicit each group's response. These become the starting point for your own observations. They also give you a good feel for how the students presently understand the notion of grace. Your comments should follow the lines developed above concerning the distinction between grace as a "thing" with rather individualistic connotations (the scotch tape arrangement) and grace as Jesus' presence, his relationship to us, his being there as friend and helper (the free agent arrangement).

You could also mention how grace as relationship

usually implies a communal effort, a kind of working together, whereas when grace is viewed as some "thing" we get to aid us individually, we do not pay that much attention to others even when we have a common purpose. In fact, we can often get upset when others do not seem to be doing their share.

Finally, a direct application should be made to a particular sacrament, for example, Matrimony, explaining how the grace is Christ's presence to the marrying couple and to the community precisely as a friend, concerned for the couple, offering help and encouragement, involving the whole community in order to bring support to the couple.

Having made your own observations it is a good idea at this point to encourage the students to ask further questions of you. Or you may ask each group to attempt now to formulate together a definition of grace, based on your comments. Each group can share their definition with the others and you would again make observations, pointing out misunderstandings, especially good definitions, etc. Since the main concern here is emphasis on grace as God's freely given presence and offer of friendship, take as much time as is necessary to insure the students grasp that concept and distinguish it from grace viewed as a "thing" received.

As an alternate or reinforcement to the above activity, either of the following activities could be used.

A Friend Is . . . This activity is less dynamic, but it gets the point across. Give each student—or group of students—the following list of statements, each to be completed with one word:

1. If I were sick a real friend would be . . .
2. If I were sad a real friend would be . . .
3. If I were happy a real friend would be . . .

4. If I were being selfish and mean a real friend would be . . .
5. If I were discouraged a real friend would be . . .
6. If I were starting a new job a real friend would be. . . .

You will want to give them an example of what you mean, such as:

If I were sick a real friend would be concerned (or sympathetic, or worried).

After each person or group completes the task, ask them to compare and comment on their results. Next ask them if they can describe what seems to be constant in any friendship despite the many forms of expression it can take. Hopefully, they will arrive at the idea of the relationship itself as one of selflessness, identity with the friend, the ongoing gift of self to another precisely because he is a friend. At some point in this kind of discussion interject the question: "Why can we call any friendship a grace?" After exploring this concept in terms of the root meaning of the word grace as a freely offered and unearned gift, ask the more direct question: "What do we mean when we say the sacraments give us grace? What is the grace we experience in any sacrament?" From the responses obtained you have a starting point for making your own comments on the nature of grace and sacrament as described above.

Film. Though the film "The Parable" has been over-used in the past, it could well be resurrected in relation to this topic. It contains in rather dramatic fashion a clear statement of the kinds of relationships Jesus has with us, each according to our particular need. Here we can "see" grace as fundamentally a relationship and not as a thing.

The procedure could take one of two directions.

You could begin with a direct presentation about the nature of grace as a relationship and then present the film as an example of what you mean. After showing it you would have some discussion and relate the concept of grace to what happens in the sacraments. Or you could begin by showing the film and by means of questions and discussion afterward lead the students to an understanding of what is meant by grace.

II. *The Next Step*

Having clarified the overall notion of grace as God's offer of himself as a friend, his presence to us, his ongoing concern for us, we want to move more directly to the idea of the particular grace of each sacrament.

This activity is not exactly what is called a dynamic but it does provide the basis for beginning a presentation or discussion. Simply provide each student—or group—with the following form:

Society Event	Friend's Relationship or Involvement	Sacrament	Jesus' Relationship or Involvement
Birth		Baptism	
Maturity		Confirmation	
Daily Living		Eucharist	
Marriage		Matrimony	
Career		Orders	
Failures		Reconciliation	
Sickness/Death		Healing	

Explain that there are certain key moments in each person's life regardless of the culture in which he lives.

In each of these moments our friends normally will "be with us" in a particular way. In the Church community we have parallel moments represented by the reception of particular sacraments. In each of these moments Jesus becomes "present to us" for a particular purpose. The task is to fill out with a descriptive word or phrase the kind of relationship or involvement we expect of friends and of Jesus in the parallel circumstances.

Results of individuals or groups can be shared and compared. Based on their own understanding of "what's happening" in each individual sacrament your own comments would then either reinforce or correct their observations. Again stress the nature of grace as Jesus' presence and his relationship to us. To further illustrate this it is a good time at this point to read several Gospel passages which illustrate Jesus "at work" in particular circumstances and how his relationship with individuals takes on slightly different emphasis in each case. Of special value are the incidents surrounding the Marriage Feast at Cana (John 2:1-12), the Repentance of Mary Magdalene (Luke 7:36ff) and/or Zacchaeus (Luke 19:1-11), Jarius' Daughter (Luke 8:41ff). Many others could be selected, of course. In any event, what we see in such passages is Jesus responding to particular needs in a way parallel to particular sacraments —in these cases, Matrimony, Forgiveness and the Sacrament of the Anointing of the Sick.

Ask the students to observe the kinds of things Jesus does, his attitudes, his style as it were. Then stress that it is the same Jesus present doing the same kinds of things in the various sacraments. It is Jesus' presence and activity in the sacraments that makes them unique, grace-filled experiences.

Some might find it more effective to reverse the

above process by first dealing with the Gospel passages and their implications regarding sacramental grace and then proceed to the exercise involving the form. Both approaches are valid.

In either case one additional concept should be stressed now. Sacraments give particular kinds of "strength," but this notion of strength must be viewed in the form of influence, not some quantitative thing.

This can be seen dramatically in the instance of Zacchaeus. He came under the influence of Jesus, he was drawn to Jesus by his warmth and love and forgiving attitude. It was this influence based on Jesus' new relationship to him that accounts for his "power" to so totally reform his life. Zacchaeus was not storing up "power," rather he was growing in a living relationship. It is the relationship that makes the difference. All else flows from this. Once having introduced this point, ask the students to recount from their own experience times when they "drew strength" from friends or parents. What were the circumstances? What happened? Was this strength something tangible or was it actually rooted in the awareness that other persons were "for you," influencing you to act differently?

If time permits you may now wish to have the students pursue with you the different kinds of "strength" each sacrament brings, that is, the kinds of influence Jesus exercises on us in each particular sacrament. This simply reinforces the concepts presented earlier, from a slightly different point of view. As alternates to these activities the following can be used:

Old Magazines. For younger students it is often more effective to use the above form with a variation. Namely, instead of having them write down the kind of relationship or involvement involved in the key moments, ask them to try to find appropriate pictures in old magazines that tend to describe what is involved. This would be followed by a kind of "show and tell" in which they explain why they chose particular pictures for particular events. This provides you with the entry needed to make the kinds of comments developed above and to pursue the topic more directly.

Find the Event. This activity serves several purposes. It will help students to root the origin of sacraments more closely with the life of Jesus while at the same time illustrating the different kinds of relationships and influences that are provided in the various sacraments. Individually or in small groups ask the students to find events in the life of Jesus that parallel what happens in each of the sacraments. Do not over-explain but do provide at least one example of what you have in mind. For instance, use the story of Jesus and Jarius' daughter as a sample of an event which parallels what is happening when we celebrate the sacrament of healing.

This will take some time, especially if they lack familiarity with the Gospels. So you could either assign it as a take-home task or you could divide the class into groups, each with one sacrament. In the latter case they would be asked to find as many instances as they can in the time allowed. When the task is completed and the reports are shared you then have the opportunity to pursue the overall topic with more direct input by yourself.

III. *The Heart of the Matter*

In a real sense this next topic is not quite as climactic as the title suggests. But since the concern here is for developing the idea of the communal nature of the sacraments as this relates to grace, the principles involved are applied to all the sacraments. In that sense at least the concepts are central to the whole unit. What we hope to provide is an experience of how every person present is or should be involved in any sacramental celebration.

Also, the greater the degree of communal involvement, the greater is the potential for experiencing Jesus' presence and activity. A simple way to do this is to form a group of eight persons, giving each a number from one to eight. Several such groups can be formed and participate simultaneously. Provide each group with a large, inflated balloon. Arrange each group in a circle in order according to their numbers. Explain that the task is to try to keep the balloon in the air at all times. The rules are these:

1. Keep one hand behind your back at all times.
2. Keep your left foot stationary at all times. You can move your right foot as necessary.
3. You cannot participate until your number is called.
4. Each group will begin with only No. 1 and No. 5 participating. You must not help until your number is called. Once called you can continue to participate until the end of the exercise.
5. If your balloon hits the floor you must stop the activity until another number is called. Then the group can begin again.
6. The group with the least number of "drops" wins.

Give a balloon to each No. 1. Signal to begin. Periodically, call another number or pair of numbers until all are participating. Continue until only one group still has the balloon in the air or until it is obvious the various groups could now continue indefinitely.

Re-form and begin to solicit observations with some of the following questions: How did No. 1 and No. 5 feel when they were working alone? How did those left watching feel? What happened when your number was finally called? How did you feel? Did the task continue to grow easier as each individual was called to participate? Any other comments?

Following these observations turn to the more direct question: What is the parallel between what we have just been doing and the celebration of a sacrament —if we consider the balloon as representative of Christ's presence and his grace in any sacrament? Hopefully, the analogies will be rather obvious to them.

If they are not forthcoming, you at least have the opportunity now to make comments of your own regarding the role of the community both in being the means through which Jesus makes his presence and friendship visible and the potential effect Jesus' presence has on *all* present.

From this kind of input you can then move on to observations or applications to particular sacraments, for example: Forgiveness, Matrimony, Baptism. The students should be asked to make their own observations about what the role of the community might be in each of these cases and the kind of effect the sacrament would have on all present.

Finally, attention should be given to the implications of this for Eucharist, for it is here that all these principles are most obviously applicable. Students could be asked to share experiences of particularly "good" Eucharists and particularly "bad" ones. What was the reason in each instance? Pursue this as long as it is profitable. As alternates the following could be used:

Reverse the Process. Here you would use the same balloon game but instead of gradually adding participants, begin with all participating and gradually reduce the number by calling out a specific number periodically. The basic effect is the same and the questions and comments would follow as described above.

Singing into Community. Using the same principle as the balloon but without the physical aspects, form groups, giving numbers, etc., as above. Numbers 1 and 5 would begin singing a well known song such as *Battle Hymn of the Republic* and the others would join as their numbers are signaled or called out. In this case there is no contest involved. Motivation would depend on the students' trust of the teacher—he or she has a good reason for asking us to go through this activity. The observations and questions would follow basically as described above.

Summary

This unit could be viewed as terminal. For that reason as much time as possible should be allowed for it, especially for the formal input by the teacher, and for questions and discussion by the students.

We are into some real theology now and the question of the nature of grace is pivotal not just to an understanding of sacraments but to the whole economy of salvation. The teacher should not be hesitant for this reason to seek some outside resources such as a guest speaker to insure that the matter is adequately covered. At the same time we cannot push too hard, especially with those in the junior high grades. Our concern is to give them an enlightened appreciation of the sacraments at this stage in their lives; we cannot hope to make them professional sacramental theologians. Even with the older students emphasis should be on appreciation first. They will have a lifetime to continue to grow in an understanding of grace, provided we can at least get them started in the right direction.

7. Seven, Eleven or Seventy-Seven

Introduction

While we have focused from time to time on particular sacraments we have been concerned basically with the sacraments from a more general point of view. Hopefully, we have suggested some ways to present these overall concepts to students. For the most part though, we have begged the question in several areas. For instance, we have presumed or taken for granted that there are seven sacraments. We have already suggested, of course, that these seven reflect certain key values of Jesus that are necessary for all human community regardless of a particular culture. But we have never really traced back to find out how the Church arrived at the precise number of seven.

Also, we have begged the question regarding the signs the Church uses in her ritual celebration of the sacraments. We have said very little about how these seven rituals were developed and adapted over the centuries.

These matters are not crucial for an appreciation of the sacraments, especially for younger students, but for the more mature and intellectually critical student an excursion into these areas will round out the understanding of sacraments.

Because of the nature of this book, we have not given a detailed history of the development of the sacraments. Rather we would like to focus our attention on a method for providing this kind of information to students. The seven sacraments as a closed system was not defined by theologians until the Middle Ages and then by the Council of Trent, in the late 16th century to be precise. This does not mean there was no strong tradition of seven sacraments prior to that. It just means it became official at that time in response to certain challenges made by Martin Luther and his followers.

In the period of the apostles and on into the first several centuries, we can find ample evidence of the practice and the development of the ritual celebration of Baptism, Confirmation, Eucharist, Orders and Anointing of the Sick. Also, there is a clear reference in John's Gospel to the establishment of the Sacrament of Forgiveness (cf. John 20:22-23) which was written toward the end of the first century. It clearly reflects the Church's awareness at that time. However, the emergence of a distinct ritual celebration of forgiveness apart from that contained with Baptism and the Eucharist is not in evidence until the third century when apostates sought re-entry into the Church. Private auricular (in the ear) confession to a priest (as opposed to confession to the bishop who was the "ordinary confessor" in the early Church) did not come into wide practice until the eighth century. In other words, there is a clear development of the understanding of the sacrament and its ritual celebration that extends over many centuries.

Likewise, with the Sacrament of Matrimony, marriage between Christians was regarded from earliest times as something special, clearly distinct from the marriage between pagans. Paul even uses the relationship between the Christian husband and wife as a symbol of the relationship Jesus has with his Church. Yet the ritual celebration of marriage was not clearly defined as sacramental until the Middle Ages.

Even with those sacraments definitely celebrated as sacraments in the early Church, there has been continuous development both in the understanding of their nature and in the form of the celebration. This is most easily seen by a casual study of the history of the Eucharist. Even during apostolic times, as the gospels and epistles were being composed, we can trace this kind of development as it moved from Jerusalem where the synagogue influenced it to the Gentile world where the agape custom became a dominant influence.

Likewise, Baptism and Confirmation underwent several phases of development as the Church moved from being primarily concerned with the conversion of adults to a time when it began to baptize infants born of Christian parents. For example, there is little or no evidence of infant Baptism in apostolic times. There is much evidence that Baptism and Confirmation, followed by Eucharist were all part of a single initiation ceremony for the adult convert. Only with time did this kind of initiation evolve into the three separate acts. Eventually, the Sacrament of Penance was interjected into the process.

Even this cursory glance at the origins and development of our sacramental system suggests that we would be pretty naive to think the sacraments are some static set of rituals fully developed and practiced by the Church shortly after the death-resurrection of Jesus and based on his precise instructions. In a real sense we can say the Church discovered the sacraments through her instinctive desire to recall the words and deeds of Jesus and to imitate his values.

That the Church eventually arrived at seven rather than eleven or seventy-seven is in one sense arbitrary. But we cannot overlook, either, the continuing role the Spirit plays in guiding the Church. From an historical point of view we can say the development of seven sacraments is somewhat accidental. From a sociological and psychological point of view it is predictable—since they reflect certain basic needs and values common to all men. From a faith-inspired, theological view we can say the number seven was foreordained by God and revealed through the work of the Spirit in the Church. In any event we do have seven ritual celebrations of Jesus' words and actions whereby we have the guaranteed opportunity to encounter Jesus himself, present and working in our midst.

What significance does this background have for us today? Primarily, it helps us to stay loose. That is, by realizing that the sacraments have undergone rather continuous development both in understanding and ritual form we can remain open to a continuing development in both areas. We will not get locked in on one particular sign or one particular aspect of a ritual to the point where a future change might upset us. Just as important, this kind of understanding helps us to focus on the real meaning and value of the sacraments as encounters with Jesus, and through him with the Father. The how and even the why of these encounters can undergo changes in understanding and celebration. What remains unchanging is that they are encounters with the living God.

If we share this kind of insight with our students

without scandalizing them into thinking the sacraments are just some more "hocus pocus" found in every religion, we have done them a big favor.

How can we do this? There is one approach I would like to suggest. It has the advantage of putting the burden primarily on the students and thus allow them to go as deeply as their present needs and capacities dictate. It is the research approach.

I. *The Research Approach: Some Options*

Motivation is the key in this approach. In a formal class where assignments are expected and grades received there is some built-in motivation. This is especially true with senior high school students who are more familiar with research projects.

In the CCD setting though, and among junior high students a straight research project will have little appeal. For that reason it is usually best to move away from the traditional "written report" project. Instead, emphasis should be placed on oral, dramatic, or graphics reports. Also, more interest can be generated by allowing persons to work in groups, permitting them to choose the particular sacrament they want to research, granting them considerable freedom in the choice of media for making their report.

Keeping in mind then that we are using research report in a more flexible and creative sense the following principles will be of some help in initiating this approach:

1. Begin by giving the students some general introduction to the fact that the sacramental system has developed over the centuries, even though the origins

for all seven sacraments can be found in both the life of Jesus and the life of the early Church.

2. Give the students a general explanation of what you mean by a research project into the origins and development of a sacrament. That is, describe the general areas of concern:

a. Basis in Scripture, particularly the New Testament.
b. How it was practiced in the early Church—from the death of Christ until about third century.
c. Any significant changes over the centuries—What? Why? Or any significant differences in the way it was practiced in particular parts of the world—What? Why?
d. What happened at the Council of Trent?
e. Any significant changes since Vatican II?

3. After providing such a prodigious sounding outline it is good to indicate immediately the kinds of resources you can make available or that can be found in the school or public library. Unless working with a particularly challenging group you normally would not expect them to get much beyond the Catholic Encyclopedia or similar standard references, the American Catechism (Herder and Herder) and the Vatican Documents.

4. Also, explain at this point the possible methods for reporting the project. Here use the ideas of flexibility and creativity just mentioned.

5. In assigning or allowing students to choose their sacrament the only concern is that every sacrament is covered by someone. It is often possible, if students work alone rather than in groups, to get several reports on each sacrament.

6. Allow sufficient time for the project—about two weeks at least. Much more time will not necessarily improve the quality of the work. Human nature being what it is, more time will only tend to postpone starting until a later date.

7. Allow sufficient time for giving the reports, especially since oral, dramatized or visualized reports will need adequate time to do them justice. Do not feel this time is being wasted. It is a valid way to achieve your objective here, namely sensitizing students to the developmental character of the sacraments and providing them with at least some background on each sacrament.

8. Obviously it is necessary for the teacher to do some research of his own on each of the sacraments in order to make observations, ask effective questions and provide any corrections necessary. *The New American Catechism* mentioned in Chapter 1 is invaluable for this purpose.

9. Finally, do not be disappointed if the quality of the report is not quite what you had hoped for, especially at the junior high level. As just stated, the objective can still be achieved even if the report is not for example quite a doctoral dissertation on the history of Confirmation.

An alternative to trying to cover all of the sacraments is to have the whole class work on one sacrament like Eucharist or Forgiveness, each person or group preparing a report on a particular period of time: Apostolic Church, from the second to sixth century, Middle Ages, Reformation, etc. Having sensitized them to how one sacrament has developed it is relatively easy to make the same kind of application to all the sacraments.

A third alternative, of course, is for you to prepare personally a presentation on the historical development of each of the sacraments and give it in a direct manner. In some instances this might be the most realistic and productive approach, but student involvement is always preferred whenever possible.

Summary

The entire content of this unit can be regarded in one sense as optional. It is largely academic and has no immediate value for many students. At the same time, as indicated above, it is important that they obtain a certain sense of relativity within tradition, a certain freedom with the "law" to counter that tendency in all of us to revert to magic in our attempt to relate to God.

Also, to pursue this topic of historical development is to help the students to become more sensitive and less critical of what they see today in the ritual celebration of many sacraments. Things are the "way they are" for a reason. It may not be a good reason for them. It does not necessarily have to be that way forever. But the conservative pastor, the uptight parent, the rather formal, inhibited celebration are not the results of bad will. More often they are the results of a particular set of historical circumstances and will only be overcome with more history, namely the history we are writing each day by our own decisions.

This kind of sensitivity to tradition, acceptance of the present and openness to the future is best achieved by gaining some kind of historical perspective. If today's youth lack anything—in my personal judgment—it is an historical perspective. If an historical treatment of the sacraments will help them to develop that perspective, that alone is a justification for the unit. If it gives them the beginnings of a perspective on the why and what of the sacraments today, I'd say the unit is essential.

of the experiments will gets them to devise that particular; that show of a direction on the one hand. It
gives distinctive beginnings of ? respective on the why
and what of the statements to say. But that is and is not
intelligible.

8. A Kind of Appendix

As a supplement to teaching individual sacraments along the lines described in Chapter 7 the following background material and suggestions are offered.

I. *Baptism*

In the Old Testament, Baptism is foreshadowed in a variety of ways. For one thing water had great symbolic value for people living in the arid Mid-East. More important, water played a central part in some of the most significant events in the history of the Hebrews. The story of the Flood (Gen. 6-9) is one such event and the idea of water being a cleansing or purgative element was not lost on the people. It became an integral part of their religious rituals of cleansing. Even more significant was the role of water in their escape from Egypt, the passage through the Red Sea and the destruction of Pharaoh's army in that same sea (Ex. 14). This is paralleled by a similar event when they finally reached the Promised Land and passed through the River Jordan (Josh. 4). Thus the symbolism of water as a saving element became deeply imbedded in the tradition of the people.

The actual practice of Baptism as a sign of conversion and the beginning of a new life style was apparently rather common by the time of John the Baptist. That he used this ritual was not considered novel by the people.

The basis for the Church adopting this ritual for such a sign of conversion and re-birth in Christ rests on various actions and words of Jesus. His own baptism by John clearly sets a precedent.

He spoke of a baptism of the Spirit (Lk. 12:50) and while it would be hard to pinpoint just when Jesus established this practice for his apostles it is clear that they began to baptize converts shortly after Jesus' resurrection and ascension. It was the accepted way of initiating persons into the community of believers. Paul, in his letters, developed the theology behind the practice, explaining the symbolism of baptism as a personal death to a life of sin and a resurrection to life in Jesus, a sacramental participation in Jesus' own death and resurrection (e.g., Rom. 6:3-11; Col. 2:8-3:17).

The actual ritual act took a variety of forms—immersion, sprinkling, and pouring—but to fully understand the ritual we have to realize that in apostolic times and in the early Church Baptism was viewed as only one part of the total initiation rite. Confirmation or the anointing with the Spirit and Eucharist were also integral. This three-part initiation rite gradually became three separate rites when the practice of infant baptism began to become widespread. This did not happen, however, until about the fifth century. Prior to that, infant baptism, though practiced, was more a local custom than a universal practice. One of the major reasons for the establishment of the practice of infant baptism was the development of a theology of original sin in response to the erroneous teachings of Pelagius, who down played the need for grace to overcome sin. So from about the fifth century on the Church baptized infants and around this practice developed a sense of urgency lest the unbaptized child die and thus be excluded from heaven.

This understanding and mentality persisted in the Church until our own day. Now, however, several things are contributing to a review of the practice of infant baptism. On the one hand we have the situation in some "Christian" countries like France where virtually every person is baptized as an infant even though the parents and adult members of the family do not practice the faith. It is more a sociological than a theological practice for such people. Therefore, some argue that it would be good to return to the practice of adult baptism which would demand a conscious conversion from a life of sin to a new life in Christ.

Also, theologians are rethinking the theology of original sin and this is having an effect on the attitude toward the urgency for infant baptism. They do not deny the reality of original sin but describe it more in terms of an evil influence or environment into which each child is born. It is not viewed as a "thing" on the soul which bars a person from heaven until it is removed. Baptism, then, is once again understood as initiation into a community of believers, initiation into a wholeness environment dominated by the spirit of Jesus.

Today, then, we could argue both ways. There are some good theological and pastoral reasons for re-establishing an adult catechumenate and for postponing Baptism until the late teens or adulthood. This is especially true in societies where the majority of people are only nominal Christians but do not practice the faith. There is equal justification for continuing the practice of infant baptism, especially in families and societies where the faith is strong. The ritual initiation of the child also reminds the adults of their duty to make Christ a reality to the child as he or she matures.

Besides the "research" approach described in Chapter 7 there are several other possible approaches for studying this sacrament. One would be the problematic approach. In this case the problem would be stated in terms of whether or not infant baptism should be continued. Students would be asked to take sides and prepare arguments pro and contra. Or they could be asked to interview others (pastor, parents, other teachers) and report their attitudes on the topic. Eventually ask each student to make a personal decision on the matter and be prepared to defend it with both theological and pastoral reasons. In this kind of problematic method students would actually become involved in the process of learning more about the whole theology of the sacrament, past practices and current opinions, as they would in a research project, but this method has the advantage of dealing with a practical type of question and the work tends to be more relevant. An alternative is to arrange for students to actually observe and/or participate in a Baptism ceremony. It would be ideal, of course, if it should happen that one of the students (with older groups) has been asked to be a godparent. As preparation for the ceremony the students could review the ritual. In this context the teacher has many opportunities to present the theological and historical background of the sacrament.

With younger children a teacher could stage a "mock" Baptism with children playing various roles— parents, priest, godparents, uncles and aunts, acolytes, choir, etc. Preparing for this kind of dramatization also gives an excellent opportunity for explaining the nature of the sacrament.

Finally, since baptism is a ritual shared by all Christian denominations this sacrament provides an opportunity for an ecumenical approach. Persons from different denominations could be asked to speak to the students about how they understand the sacrament and how it is celebrated. Or students could be asked to interview ministers or adult acquaintances of other denominations on the subject and report back to the whole group. In the process the teacher can talk of similarities and differences between the Catholic tradition and the other traditions.

II. *Confirmation*

In Old Testament literature the Spirit of God did not have the personification that Christ revealed, but there are many references to the power of God or his Spirit and the effect on men when they came under the influence of God's Spirit. The prophets, for example, were generally considered capable of their deeds and words because they were seized by the Spirit of God.

Jesus speaks much more directly of the Spirit as person and the real basis for Confirmation lies in his promise to send the Spirit upon his followers (Lk. 24:29). Historically, this took place on the first Pentecost and the results of the outpouring of the Spirit are described in Acts 2.

The Acts of the Apostles have preserved two very significant episodes which attest to further action of the Spirit: the incident of Philip the deacon preaching in Samaria, etc., (Acts 8:4-8, 14-17) and the laying on of hands by Paul at Ephesus (Acts 19:1-6).

These texts point out that after Baptism of water was a second rite—the imposition of hands—by which the newly baptized received the Holy Spirit. This second rite was reserved to the apostles. The initiation rite, begun with Baptism, was completed with the gift of the Holy Spirit, a gift that might be accompanied by sensible manifestations such as speaking in tongues and prophecy. Moreover, the events of Pentecost were the sensible manifestations of the coming upon the apostles of that plenitude of the Spirit that Jesus had promised (Acts 1:4-5, 8; 2:1-7; 10:44-47).

There was then a new gift of the Spirit, distinct from that of Baptism, which was realized by the imposition of the apostle's hands. Thus the Acts bring the successive phases of Christian initiation to our knowledge; preaching and conversion, Baptism of water, and imposition of hands that gives the Spirit. It is important to remember that, barring few exceptions, the early Church of the Acts usually baptized only adults. Christianity was viewed more as an adult religion with adult responsibility.

There is a lacuna in the documentation on the existence after apostolic times of a second sacrament distinct from Baptism. One cannot cite in favor of it the few allusions to an anointing made by St. Justin or by Theophilus of Antioch, for they can be understood in a purely metaphorical sense. However, the existence of a second rite complementary to Baptism from the third century on is clearly attested everywhere. Tertullian knew of a post-Baptismal anointing and imposition of hands that called down the Holy Spirit in Africa; St. Hippolytus in his *Apostolic Tradition* gives a complete description of Baptismal rites: an anointing with "oil of exorcism," the triple immersion, an anointing with "sanctified oil" by the priest, the imposition of the bishop's hands, followed by another anointing with sanctified oil by the "consignation" on the forehead.

The fourth and fifth centuries offer equally numerous and clear evidences for the sacramentality of Confirmation. Thus the Church in this period knew and practiced universally a complex rite of initiation that was essentially composed of Baptism of water, followed by an anointing or imposition of hands or both. In this richly symbolic rite it is not always so easy to distinguish what pertained to Baptism from what belonged to the second sacrament we call Confirmation. Where did Baptism end and where did Confirmation begin? Perhaps we should not try to distinguish too precisely, for we are dealing with a single rite, the various elements of which followed each other without interruption. It is to be noted, however, that the final ceremony, the imposition of hands or anointing was normally reserved to the bishop, and that by this rite the Christian was said to be completed, "perfected" by the gift of the Holy Spirit.

During the period of the catechumenate and the evolution of the Lenten season and the Easter Vigil Liturgy we see a blending of the three elements into a full "initiation rite." At the end of Lent, after going through the catechumenate, a person would be accepted into the Church. The two parts of the ceremony, Baptism of water and anointing of the Spirit were still united. Then, the newly baptized attended the full liturgy of the Eucharist for the first time. These three steps are known as the full rite of initiation into Christianity. At this time, the second step was called "consignation" and was done by the local bishop after a priest had conferred the Baptism of water.

There seem to be two major considerations besides

the Pelagian heresy that decided the separation of the three sacraments into separate sacramental rites. One was the increase in the number of people seeking admission into the Church and the difficulty for the bishop to be present at every adult Baptism. Another was the parental concern for children. Infant mortality rates were high and the practice of infant baptism became widespread. Soon it was the prevailing practice. Again, the bishop just could not be present at so many occasions.

Thus, by the fifth century Pope Innocent I clearly distinguished the rite of "consignation" from the baptismal anointing and from Baptism itself. Thereafter, Confirmation was a distinct rite in the entirety of sacramental rites. In the twelfth century when theologians began to list the seven sacraments, or major rites that are efficacious signs of grace, Confirmation came after Baptism. The doctrine was made definite at the Council of Lyons in 1274.

Since the time of the Council of Trent, Confirmation was conferred at about the age of twelve within the Western Church. Before this century Communion was received for the first time shortly after Confirmation, keeping the sequence intact: Baptism, Confirmation, Eucharist.

In 1910, St. Pope Pius X decreed that children might receive Communion as early as the age of seven and this broke the customary sequence. Rome tried without success to have the practice of Confirmation changed. It was Vatican II that called for a new rite of Confirmation. The new rite was promulgated in September 1971.

The one sacrament that has suffered the most disruption, wrenched from its early Christian context and almost completely redirected, is the sacrament of Confirmation. So the fathers at Vatican II stated in the Constitution on the Liturgy: The rite of Confirmation is to be revised and the intimate connection which this sacrament has with the whole of Christian initiation is to be more clearly set forth; for this reason, it is fitting for candidates to renew their baptismal promises just before they are confirmed. Confirmation may be given within Mass . . . (Article 71).

Pope Paul writes in his Apostolic Constitution on the Sacrament of Confirmation: "From ancient times the conferring of the gift of the Holy Spirit has been carried out in the Church with various rites. These rites underwent many changes in the East and in the West, while ever keeping the significance of a conferring of the Holy Spirit."

There is still much theological debate on various aspects of the sacrament of Confirmation. However, a few central ideas seem to be agreed upon.

1. CONFIRMATION IS A GIVING OF THE HOLY SPIRIT TO THOSE ALREADY BAP-TIZED.
   "Receive the seal of the Holy Spirit, the gift of the Father" - is the new essential form for the sacrament established by Pope Paul VI on August 15, 1971.
2. CONFIRMATION IS RELATED TO BAPTISM AND THE EUCHARIST AND ALL THREE, IN-TERRELATED, ARE PARTS OF AN ORGANIC WHOLE WHICH IS THE CHRISTIAN INITIA-TION RITE.
   After a brief review of the interrelationship between the Holy Spirit and Christ in the New Testament, Pope Paul writes: "This makes clear the specific im-

portance of Confirmation for the sacramental initiation whereby the faithful "as members of the living Christ, are incorporated into Him and made like unto Him through Baptism, Confirmation and the Eucharist."

In Baptism, neophytes receive forgiveness of sins, adoption as sons of God and the character of Christ, whereby they are made members of the Church and given a first sharing in the priesthood of their Savior (cfr. I Pet. 2, 5-9). Through the sacrament of Confirmation, those who have been born anew in Baptism receive the inexpressible Gift, the Holy Spirit himself, by which "they are endowed . . . with special strength." Moreover, having received the character of this sacrament, they are "bound more intimately to the Church" and "they are strictly obliged to spread and defend the faith both by word and by deed as true witnesses of Christ."

Finally, Confirmation is so closely linked with the Holy Eucharist that the faithful, after being signed by holy Baptism and Confirmation, are incorporated fully into the Body of Christ by participation in the Eucharist. (Apostolic Constitution on Confirmation)

3. THE GIFT OF THE SPIRIT IS A STRENGTHENING

"In the gift of the Spirit, 'they (the confirmed) are endowed . . . with special strength.' "
(Apostolic Constitution)

4. CONFIRMATION CALLS FOR WITNESS

"Having received the character of this sacrament, they (the confirmed) are 'bound more intimately to the Church' and 'are strictly obliged to spread and defend the faith both by word and by deed as true witnesses of Christ.' " (Apostolic Constitution)

In terms of study, this sacrament offers a unique opportunity in that the child is normally more mature than when preparing for first Communion and first Penance. Also, it is becoming more and more common for dioceses to postpone Confirmation until the late teens. As a result, the best way and the best time to study this sacrament is when preparing to receive it. There is usually more motivation among students and this is supported by parental involvement.

When presenting this sacrament to a group who have already been confirmed for several years, as is still often the case when working with senior high students, the best approach is to plan a para-liturgical renewal of the Confirmation commitment. This could be celebrated in conjunction with graduation for example, or within a liturgy ending the school year. The task in these instances is to review with the students what Confirmation means and the kinds of responsibilities and support the sacrament brings to them as they continue to mature as Christians. This also provides an opportunity to review the nature of the sacraments in general.

III. *Penance*

The theme of God's forgiveness runs throughout the Old Testament and the Hebrew people had various religious rituals of cleansing reparation for those who transgressed the Covenant. But the sacrament of Penance (Forgiveness, Reconciliation) is not ritually foreshadowed in the Old Testament in the same manner as are some of the other sacraments, like Baptism, whose scriptural basis is usually rooted in Jn. 20:21-23 when on the first Easter Jesus gives the apostles the power to forgive sins. He bestows this power on them after God had conquered sin and death through Jesus' death and resurrection. In a real sense, then, the whole New Testament is the story of God's forgiving the sins of mankind. The Church's first mission was to announce this forgiveness, call people to conversion and baptize them into the life of Jesus. In other words, the Church's power to forgive sins was first seen as being exercised in baptizing, the primary sacrament of reconciliation.

However, it soon became obvious that not everyone who was baptized remained faithful to the ideals of the Christian life. As a result the Church realized the necessity of providing persons with a second chance if they had fallen back into pagan ways. This kind of reconversion ritual was initially required only for serious public offenses (murder, apostasy, open adultery) and was very rigid. A person would have to submit himself to the bishop who would impose a public penance, sometimes lasting years. The rest of the Church was instructed to pray for the person, who was barred from the congregation and the liturgy until the penance was fulfilled. At the appointed time the bishop would readmit the person to Eucharist. It should be noted that such a ritual reconversion was allowed by the Church *only once* in each person's lifetime after Baptism. As might be expected people began to put off such a reconciliation ritual until late in life for fear that they might fall into sin again while young. Also the very rigor of the ritual tended to drive people away. The practice all but disappeared by the sixth century.

At that time, though, another movement began which eventually resulted in a form of sacramental ritual much more like what we ourselves have come to know as Penance. It began as a practice among Irish monks of confiding in a spiritual father or director in order to root out faults and grow in holiness. Penances were advised to correct these faults. Gradually this practice expanded to lay persons around the monasteries who sought out the advice of spiritual fathers. Irish missionaries introduced this practice to the rest of Europe, together with penitential handbooks which assigned particular penances to particular sins. In this way private confession developed and replaced the former public ritual of reconciliation. Priests became the ordinary ministers. The practice of frequent confession was urged and by the thirteenth century it became mandatory for Catholics guilty of serious sin to confess at least once a year. Except in very rare instances, the ritual of public reconciliation ceased.

An important shift in emphasis should be noted in this transition from public penance to private confession. In the early Church the stress was on the works of penance (fasting, etc.) and these had to precede reconciliation. As the sacrament took on the form of private confession the emphasis began to be placed on the act of confessing and the absolution by the priest. The assigned works of penance became more lenient and a person could approach the Eucharist before they were completed.

In our own time there has been a marked decline in the number of people who approach the sacrament of Penance with any regularity. There are various reasons for this, but no one challenges the the authenticity or value of Penance as a sacrament of reconciliation for persons in serious sin. What is being challenged, it seems, is what constitutes serious or mortal sin. Some theologians argue that mortal sin is actually quite rare, especially for young children since it implies a radical change in life-style, a complete break with God. This kind of thinking is closer to the mind of the early Church and explains why the sacrament was not widely practiced in the early Church.

On the other hand, there is an argument for more frequent celebration of the sacrament centering on man's continuing need for conversion and the kind of help frequent confession can provide because of its sacramental nature.

Another aspect today is the growing practice of communal penance services which may or may not include private confession. This has a value in stressing our common need for ongoing conversion, but it de-emphasizes the "shopping list" approach to sin, confession and penance which had reduced the sacrament to a rather meaningless, mechanical ritual in the past.

The method for teaching this sacrament to students will depend to a large extent on their age and their present attitude toward it. From junior high school onward youth tend to become very self-conscious and the idea of private confession becomes very frightening, especially when it comes to matters of purity. Much also depends on the students' present understanding of sin. For these reasons it is often best to begin by having the students express their present attitudes about the sacrament and their understanding of what sin is. This could be done by anonymous questionnaires, open discussion, group discussion, gestalting. Their feelings could also be expressed in symbolic ways (the collage, paper sculpture, drawings, etc.).

In response to this information from the students, the teacher can present an overview of the historical development of the ritual and also confront the question of sin, sinfulness, conversion and reconciliation.

This should be followed by asking the students to

develop in groups what they think would be an appropriate "examination" with them, observing any misconceptions about the nature of sin. Here it is important to help the students to become realistic without becoming scrupulous. It should be stressed that mortal sin is a radical break with God, and that it involves one's whole life-style. Mortal sin is more often a *pattern* of life than one single act.

As the students refine their understanding of sin and sinfulness, the next step would be to ask them to help develop a communal penance service appropriate for dealing with the "sins" of their age group. It should be planned in such a way as to provide the opportunity for sacramental confession, but the stress should be kept on the communal aspects of the celebration.

In the process of planning, the teacher has another opportunity to clarify the nature of the sacrament, the nature of sinfulness and reconciliation, the nature of personal conversion and penance. One point to stress is the overall nature of sacraments which centers on the presence of Christ and his action in our midst through the ritual signs. It is always he who forgives, heals, strengthens—and this is the ultimate reason for the sacramental celebration of Penance.

An alternate to this approach is the problematic approach described above. Here the problem should focus on whether or not confession of sins is necessary for forgiveness. Groups both pro and contra should be formed and asked to develop arguments for their position. In the process of their work and the resulting reports, the teacher will have ample opportunity for dealing with the topics just mentioned. Again, the celebration of a communal penance service should be included at the end.

IV. *Marriage*

Normally it is not necessary to deal with this subject in any depth until the latter terms of high school. Then it should be treated as a special topic and sufficient time should be allowed for it. This usually takes the form of a marriage preparation course, a central part of which is the sacramental character of Christian marriage. A variety of text books and manuals are available for use in presenting such a course. In treating it prior to such an in-depth course, most discussion will usually focus on the problem of indissolubility and divorce. In a typical class of thirty students there will be at least one student whose parents are divorced. For that reason the topic must be presented with sensitivity. Current debate on this subject takes several directions. Some argue that Christ's words "What God has joined together . . ." were intended as an ideal that allowed for exceptions in our imperfect world. They support this view with the fact that the Eastern Church adopted a tolerant view of divorce and remarriage.

Others dwell more on the nature of the sacrament as covenant and stress the maturity, level of faith and understanding that persons bring to the sacramental celebration. They reason that many marriages, even though joined during the sacramental ritual, do not in fact have a sacramental character. The persons were too immature psychologically or spiritually to effect the kind of covenant the sacrament implies. Hence, their marriage can be dissolved because it doesn't fall under the dictum "What *God* has joined together. . . ." It was only a civil marriage in reality and not sacramental.

In pastoral practice, the Church has become more tolerant than in the past, while maintaining the basic tenet of the indissolubility of sacramental marriage. But there is still much discussion and a wide variety of interpretations of such things as "the internal forum." So I hesitate here to attempt anything definitive. I can only suggest that the teacher inquire about what is being done in his or her own diocese and present this information to the students.

All of this, of course, is negative. But in dealing with this very real and practical problem many opportunities present themselves for explaining the positive nature of the sacrament: that Jesus himself enters into the relationship, that it is a covenant of love and not just a legal contract, that the grace of the sacrament (Jesus' presence) is ongoing. Some of this will be wasted on younger students, but it is good to plant these seeds of the beauty and creativity of authentic sacramental marriage.

V. *Orders*

There has been much research in recent years regarding the origin and development of this sacrament—so much in fact that we can hardly do justice to it in a book of this nature. But we can at least sketch out the key ideas.

First, in the early Church there was no priesthood in the exact way we understand it today. Rather, people thought in terms of ministries, particular services within the Church for which persons had the gift and responsibility (1 Cor. 12:27-29). These ministries were first supervised by the apostles and then by a group of elders or presbyters appointed by the apostles.

It should be noted that in the early Church there

seemed to be a great deal of flexibility as to who presided over the Eucharist. This function was not identified as a unique ministry. Presiding at the liturgy did not have the aura of mystery or special power we have come to place in it. Jesus was the only High Priest and it was always he who offered the sacrifice in the minds of the people.

What was special was the ministry of evangelization and preaching. Those commissioned by the apostles to assume this ministry were designated by the laying on of hands and began to be viewed as somewhat set apart from the others—for this special work. As long as the apostles lived, local churches were under their direction. When they had died, this direction passed on to those they had commissioned and these were assisted in their task by the local groups of elders. While there are many other subtleties involved here, this became the basis for what we now understand as bishops (successors of the apostles) and priests who participate in the work of the bishop.

In the early Church this *work* was still understood in terms of proclaiming the Gospel and preserving the unity of the Church. By the third century, though, the cultic work of presiding over liturgy began to fall exclusively to those who had entered the order (community, ranks) of the apostolic successors and their presbyters. The rite for entering this order included the laying on of hands and prayer. As those in this order began to assume this cultic role more stringent moral demands were made upon them. Gradually this included celibacy and those entering into this order became viewed as a special class, sacral priests set apart for presiding at the liturgy, as well as for preaching and governing the local communities. They had received "Sacred Orders."

A variety of influences, some theological others sociological, continued this process of identifying ministry almost exclusively with ordination and ordination with the power to consecrate the host in Eucharist. One was the rise of religious communities of monks who did not serve any local church but were ordained to the priesthood and celebrated the Eucharist in private. Another was the magical character that began to surround the sacraments in general. This kind of superstition was logically transferred to the men with the power to administer the sacraments.

In the time of the Reformation, this understanding of priesthood was challenged and the reformers attempted to restore the New Testament concept of ministry, especially ministry of the Word as central to the concept of priesthood. In the process they challenged the sacramental character of ordination. The Church defended this sacramental character, but also began to restore to the concept of priesthood the concept of the ministry of the Word and other pastoral works.

In our own day two trends can be observed. First, there is an effort to remove some of the restrictions surrounding orders, such as mandatory celibacy. Behind this trend is the desire to disassemble the clerical culture that has set priests apart from the people. A second trend is the renewed awareness of the priesthood of the people and its consequent responsibility to participate in ministry, as it was understood in the early Church, a ministry that did not require sacramental orders.

As can be seen by even this brief outline, the sacrament of orders is complex, touching on many other theological areas. In teaching this sacrament to students, it usually is not necessary to try to cover all areas. Focus instead on the nature of the priesthood of the faithful. Then develop the idea of ministry as both gift and as service to the community. Finally, in this overall context of ministry sacred orders can be presented as the Church's public ratification of certain persons as ministers within the Church. One of their ministries is liturgical but it is important to stress that the role of the ordained minister goes beyond cultic priesthood and is actually rooted in Christ's commission of the apostles as proclaimers of the Gospel.

One possible method for approaching this subject is to ask a panel of several priests to discuss with the students what orders means for them personally. Such a discussion usually provides a variety of points of view and introduces the youth to the complex nature of the sacrament. Hopefully, it will also dispel certain stereotypes, both theological and cultural.

VI. *Anointing of the Sick*

The scriptural basis for this sacrament is scant in terms of direct references. James' Epistle (5:14-15) is the only direct statement about anointing the sick. However, the whole life of Jesus and the consequent work of the apostles clearly roots concern for the sick —physically, mentally, spiritually—at the center of the life of the Church.

By the fifth century we can find references to the Church's ritual practice of blessing the oil to be used for anointing the sick. By the ninth century this practice was judged to be sacramental in character. But there was one important shift in emphasis. Whereas in the early Church concern was for the sick, the Church in the

Middle Ages began to regard it more as a sacrament for the dying—hence the term Extreme Unction.

In our own day, however, the sacrament is being re-established as the sacrament for the sick and is being administered much more freely, not just to the dying but to any persons afflicted with serious though not mortal illness or other infirmity. Also, the renewed ritual provides for communal anointings and this practice is becoming popular in nursing homes and in parishes. The elderly and infirm, together with their families gather to celebrate the sacrament. That is a far cry from that fearful sight of the priest, rushing with serious countenance down a hospital corridor or driving up to a neighbor's house in great haste.

In teaching this sacrament it would be good to have the students read through the new ritual or even better to have them attend one of the communal celebrations if that is possible. It would be the simplest way to implant in their minds the compassionate and hopeful nature of this sacrament, which is in one sense the most humane of them all.

It would be good in the context of presenting this sacrament to raise up the whole question of healing, one that has received much more attention today because of the charismatic renewal. Science and parapsychology too have much to say on the subject today. Also, this sacrament suggests the warmth, concern and compassion of Jesus and this point should be explored. That this should have become one of only seven sacraments indicates the kind of person Jesus is and the occasions at which he desires to be present to us.

Conclusion

The Eucharist is noticeable by its absence in this chapter. However, since the earlier chapters focused on that sacrament there seems little need to go into it any further here.

It is hoped though that the information in this chapter does provide a starting point for treating of the individual sacraments without demanding too much supplementary study by the teacher. It only remains to repeat the advice given in the Introduction. Nothing teaches the sacraments better than their celebration. At the same time, for celebration to be effective some basic understanding is necessary. May this book help teachers and parents provide that understanding.